C

Baseball
Economics and
Public Policy

Baseball Economics and Public Policy

Jesse W. Markham
Harvard University
Paul V. Teplitz
Cambridge Research Institute

LexingtonBooks
D.C. Heath and Company
Lexington, Massachusetts
Toronto

Library of Congress Cataloging in Publication Data

Markham, Jesse William, 1916-
    Baseball economics and public policy.

    Bibliography: p.
    1. Baseball—Economic aspects—United States. 2. Baseball—Law and
legislation—United States. 3. Antitrust law—United States. I. Teplitz, Paul
V., joint author. II. Title.
GV880.M37   338.4'7796357'0973   79-6032
ISBN 0-669-03607-2

Second printing, February 1982

Published simultaneously in Canada

Printed in the United States of America

International Standard Book Number: 0-669-03607-2

Library of Congress Catalog Card Number: 79-6032

Contents

List of Figures

List of Tables

Foreword

By Resolution dated April 18, 1976, the U.S. House of Representatives established the Select Committee on Professional Sports, whose purpose it was to investigate the stability of the country's major sports industries and report on the need for legislation. The Committee, (commonly known as the "Sisk Committee," after its chairman, Hon. B.F. Sisk), issued a final report on January 3, 1977, which reviewed current developments in professional sports but did not contain any specific legislative proposals.

The Sisk Committee did, however, recommend the establishment of a successor sports oversight committee to conduct an industry-wide economic analysis of professional sports and a study of the impact of the antitrust laws and policies on professional sports operations. In response to that suggestion, major-league baseball commissioned an indepth study of its finances and operations, now published as *Baseball Economics and Public Policy*. We were fortunate indeed that a man of the reputation and ability of Professor Jesse Markham was interested in heading up a group of dedicated professionals from Cambridge Research Institute in this effort.

This book was prepared in anticipation of a 1977-1978 Congressional inquiry and its contents reflect this fact. The expected inquiry did not occur, but it should nonetheless be useful to now disseminate the work as a comprehensive and detailed economic analysis of the baseball industry at the close of 1978. This does not necessarily mean that baseball concurs with all of the conclusions reached, but certainly a scholarly work of this kind deserves public attention.

Certainly there have been changes in baseball over the past two years, including a new collective bargaining agreement with the Major League Baseball Players Association, but the basic operation of baseball as an industry has not changed. This book expertly and independently scrutinizes the entirety of baseball's economic operations, covering such topics as its organizational structure, overall financial position, ownership incentives, marketing potential, pricing policies, tax implications and, to a lesser extent, labor relations activities. This candid look at the business of baseball shows that the industry does not exercise monopoly power to the detriment of the American public. More precisely, this book answers with a clear negative the question of need for remedial antitrust sports legislation with respect to baseball.

Baseball is a vibrant and exciting competitor in the entertainment industry. More than that, it is a sport whose history is truly identified with the history of America. This book illustrates to the nation that baseball does not operate contrary to those policies and laws that serve the public good.

Bowie K. Kuhn
Commissioner of Baseball

Preface and Acknowledgments

The proper application of the nation's antitrust laws to professional baseball has been the subject of debate since the Court in 1914 declared in *American League Baseball Club* v. *Chase* (149 N.Y.S. 6) that baseball was not subject to the Sherman Act because:

> Baseball is an amusement, a sport, a game that comes clearly within the civil and criminal law of the state, and is not a commodity or an article of merchandise subject to the regulation of Congress.

Six years later Justice Holmes, speaking for the Supreme Court of the United States, affirmed the *Chase* dictum in the landmark *Federal Baseball* v. *National League* case (259 U.S. 200). Although challenged with considerable frequency over the ensuing years, the courts have consistently upheld the *Federal Baseball Club* decision on the grounds that "Congress had no intention of including the business of baseball within the scope of the federal antitrust laws" (346 U.S. 356, 1953), otherwise they would have acted to overrule the doctrine upheld in the courts. Thus was born what has come to be called the baseball anomaly—the vast and complicated body of our antitrust statutory and case law that is applicable to business generally, and to other professional sports, does not extend to professional baseball.

While Congress has not acted to overturn the courts, it has subjected the antitrust immunity of baseball to intense scrutiny for more than two decades. Among the matters of Congressional interest have been the player allocation systems, the league rules governing broadcast rights, and the creation, movement, and sale of club franchises. In 1976 the U.S. House of Representatives established the Select Committee on Professional Sports to investigate these and related matters and report on the need for legislation. In 1977 the committee issued a lengthy report addressing these antitrust issues; the report proposed no new legislation.

This study was conducted between March of 1977 and the summer of 1978 in anticipation of testimony before the Select Committee concerning possible legislation to overturn the Supreme Court's *Federal Baseball* decision, or otherwise to change baseball's antitrust status. As events unfolded, congressional agendas changed, and the hearings were not held. However, the study had proceeded along the lines familiar to economists specializing in industrial organization, focusing on the structure, conduct, and performance of professional baseball as an industry. The result was a booklength manuscript containing factual analyses that we felt would be of interest to the larger public that follows baseball as well as to those having a narrower professional interest in the antitrust issues. Particularly, we hope that the study will help dispel some of the myths and common misunderstandings that abound concerning the economics of major-league baseball.

In editing the report for publication, we have made occasional changes to reflect recent events, but in general we have not attempted to incorporate data for the last two years. However, all the evidence suggests a steady continuation of the economic patterns identified in the original study. For those readers interested in tracking the economics of baseball more recently, we have included as Appendix E a financial survey covering clubs' finances through the 1979 season.

In conducting a study of this scope and depth we have incurred obligations to a great many people. Within the professional baseball community we have been aided by Ruly Carpenter and William Giles of the Philadelphia Phillies, John Fetzer of the Detroit Tigers, Allen H. Selig of the Milwaukee Brewers, Bing Devine of the St. Louis Cardinals, John Harrington of the Boston Red Sox, Ralph Miller of the St. Petersburg Cardinals, and Henry Peters of the Baltimore Orioles. Altogether, our field work in the baseball community included conferences with eleven major-league club owners and officials, the management of two minor-league clubs, the present and former executive directors of the Major League Baseball Player Relations Committee, the president of the National Association of Professional Baseball Leagues, and various other officials, staff members, coaches, and consultants associated with baseball.

We wish to extend our special thanks to Bowie K. Kuhn, Commissioner of Baseball, for his continuing interest and support.

Others who have assisted in the research going into the study include Dr. Hazel Denton, Jesse W. Markham, Jr., Dr. Bertrand Fox, Jerry Simon, Linda Wood, David McNeal, and Elizabeth Huard, all of whom served as full-time or part-time members of the Cambridge Research Institute staff while the research was in progress. Professor Markham would like to acknowledge his debt to the Division of Research of the Harvard Business School, which provided time for a portion of his research in the final stages of drafting the manuscript.

Finally, we wish to give special thanks to our wives, Penny Markham and Kathy Teplitz, for their forebearance in becoming a special breed of "baseball widow" during our work on this study.

Baseball
Economics and
Public Policy

1 Introduction

In December 1976, the House Select Committee on Professional Sports, after months of investigation, issued a lengthy report calling for a number of reforms in the way in which professional sports in the United States are governed.[1] The report also stated that the committee's work was unfinished, and it called for further studies of professional sports, including the appointment of a successor committee in the next Congress to conduct additional investigative hearings.

One of the principal questions addressed by the Sisk committee—and one of those left unanswered—was whether organized baseball, uniquely among the professional sports, should continue to remain exempt from the antitrust laws of the United States. The committee stated:

> During the brief life-span of the Committee, it was not possible to compile sufficient information to determine what need, if any, professional sports have for special antitrust modifications or treatment. Based upon the information available to it, the Committee has concluded that adequate justification does not exist for baseball's special exemption from the antitrust laws and that its exemption should be removed in the context of overall sports antitrust reform. However, the Committee is not transmitting its recommendation on baseball's antitrust exemption to the House Judiciary Committee at this time. . . .
>
> The Committee recommends that a successor sports oversight and investigation committee be established with full authority to conduct inquiries into the need for legislation with respect to all professional sports. The mandate of the Committee should specifically direct that it conduct (1) an industry-wide economic analysis and (2) a comprehensive study to determine the impact of current antitrust law and policy on all professional sports.[2]

The committee further observed that

> there is a need for a complete understanding of the economics of the industry. For too long the Congress has considered and/or adopted legislation directly or indirectly affecting the sports industry without certainty as to its ramifications. This has been true as to legislation considered both beneficial and detrimental to the industry. Finally, it would seem equitable to explore thoroughly the possible alternatives to the present player allocation and marketing rules in professional sports.[3]

This book on the economics of baseball attempts to respond to the Sisk Committee's quest for a better understanding of the sport.

Although a successor committee was not created,[4] baseball's treatment under the antitrust laws remains an open and active question, primarily because of a 1972 ruling of the U.S. Supreme Court: "And what the Court said in *Federal Baseball* in 1922 and what it said in *Toolson* in 1953, we say again here in 1972: the remedy, if any is indicated, is for congressional, and not judicial action."[5]

Besides the question of *whether* baseball requires special treatment under the antitrust laws, there has also been disagreement as to *who* would most appropriately effect a change in baseball's status. This problem has existed for almost thirty years. As early as 1950, the House Judiciary Committee (the Celler committee) conducted hearings on the special status of baseball, and there have been hearings in many sessions of Congress since then. No major legislation has resulted. Yet, in private lawsuits dating to even earlier days, the federal courts have refused to decide the issue, stating that baseball's status could be changed only by legislation. However, undoubtedly some of the reluctance to act on the antitrust immunity has also resulted from the recognition that there *is* something peculiar about the business of a professional sport which distinguishes it from other enterprises.

The central purpose of this book is to define these peculiarities, to relate them to antitrust principles, and to analyze the possible consequences for baseball if the antitrust immunity were eliminated. This analysis is greatly aided by the availability of comprehensive financial information that provides a basis for an economic analysis of baseball as an "industry."

It should be observed that although baseball's antitrust status may be an anomaly, those practices that are usually attacked differ little from those in use throughout professional sports. Not only are the most controversial practices widespread, but also their very prevalence suggests they may be essential to the operation of a league sport.

Under ordinary application of antitrust principles, the operational aspects of baseball and other sports—player contracting, franchise allocation, territorial exclusivities, and broadcasting—are unusual. These practices raise antitrust issues because they are regulated by joint agreements among league members, rules which some critics characterize as "agreements in restraint of trade." Since much of the following discussion relates to these practices, a brief description of the more important ones is in order.

1. *Player contracting* differs from the hiring practices of most employers in two important ways. First, most sports use some form of *reverse-order draft* for allocating rookie players among teams. Teams are given, in reverse order of their league standings, exclusive (or preferred)

rights of negotiating with these players. Second, leagues employ various mechanisms to limit the ability of a player to leave one team and seek employment with another. In baseball, this mechanism is called the *reserve system,* whereby a club can reserve continuing rights to employ a player, and other clubs cannot negotiate with him until that reservation is relinquished.[6] From an antitrust point of view, these rules have been highly controversial because they represent an agreement not to compete (or to compete in only limited ways) in the purchase of player services.

2. *Franchise allocation* is an issue because new teams cannot enter a league sport on their own. They must be granted a "franchise" by the existing league members (or get enough teams together to start a new league). In baseball, such approval to enter requires a three-fourths vote in the American League or a unanimous vote in the National League. If a prospective entrant fails to receive this approval, there are no avenues for appeal.

3. *Exclusive territories* are granted by most leagues to their members, meaning that no competing teams will be located within some specified distance of an existing club. In baseball, the National League grants territorial exclusivity to its clubs within the city limits of the home city and the area within 10 miles in all directions from the city limits, while in the American League establishment of a club within 100 miles of an existing club requires consent of the latter. As for interleague locations, a club of one league may locate in a city already occupied by the other league, provided its ball park is at least 5 miles distant from the park of the preexisting club and, for cities with a population of less than 2,400,000, that three-quarters of the teams comprising the league already represented in the city approve. For larger cities, this approval is not necessary.

4. Most leagues *pool the sale of national broadcasting* rights, a practice which some observers claim is nothing more than a device for restricting broadcasters' access to games and thereby raising the price. In 1961, Congress specifically exempted certain pooled sales of broadcasting rights from antitrust laws.

The congressional committees and courts appear to have recognized that league sports are unusual economic enterprises and that these practices are not restraints of trade in the classical sense of the term.[7] The growth of players' collective-bargaining powers and headlines announcing multi-million-dollar contracts in recent years have quieted some of the earlier criticisms of professional sports. However, the special league agreements have continued to cause debate, on both conceptual and practical grounds, because of their apparent conflict with other public goals, such as due process, individuals' rights, and free and open competition.

The courts and Congress appear also to have recognized the public value of preserving professional sports as the United States knows them. They were concerned, as the Sisk committee noted, by uncertainty regarding the effects that antitrust laws might have on baseball. A contributing factor to this uncertainty has been a dearth of publicly available information on the economics of baseball.

This book seeks to address these issues in two ways. The first is by examining the conceptual foundations on which antitrust principles are based and their relationship to the peculiar characteristics of league sports. The second is through empirical research, principally a detailed analysis of baseball clubs' finances. We also investigate the process of player development, player-compensation patterns and the effects of baseball's new collective-bargaining agreement, and factors affecting the attendance of baseball clubs. (Appendix A describes more fully the sources used in this book.)

Throughout this book we have tried to keep in mind that its purpose is to offer insight into the underlying fundamentals of baseball, and not to pass judgment on specific actions or practices. In economic terms our discussion emphasizes structure, because we believe that it is the structural aspects of baseball—and of league sports generally—that have been least understood in the debate concerning sports and antitrust.

Chapter 2 briefly reviews the history of baseball's antitrust immunity. It then examines the economic principles on which the nation's antitrust policies are based and how they would appear to apply to baseball. Chapter 3 discusses the unique characteristics of league sports and what makes them different from other economic enterprises.

Chapter 4 presents empirical material on the structure of organized baseball and such matters as the flow of funds through this structure, the pattern of player compensation, and factors affecting the market for baseball games. Chapter 5 continues the empirical presentation with material on the financial performance of baseball clubs.

Finally, chapter 6 summarizes our key findings and develops an informed speculation regarding the possible implications of a loss of baseball's antitrust immunity.

Notes

1. U.S. Congress, House, Select Committee on Professional Sports, *Final Report* (Washington: USGPO, 1976). This committee was also known as the Sisk committee after its chairman, Hon. B.F. Sisk (D., Calif.).

2. Ibid., pp. 4, 7.

3. Ibid., p. 59

4. In March 1977, as part of an effort to ease members' workloads, the House voted not to reestablish a number of committees, including the special one on professional sports. The House Judiciary Committee announced that it would look into professional sports in its forthcoming consideration of all major antitrust immunities.

5. Flood v. Kuhn, 407 U.S. 258, 285 (1972).

6. Under the current collective-bargaining agreement, this reserve privilege extends only through the first five years of a player's major-league career. Prior to 1976, a club could reserve a player for his entire professional career. (Later sections of this book describe the mechanics of the reserve system.)

7. A few months after their committee finished its report (March 30, 1977), Congressmen Sisk and Horton sent a letter to the chairman and ranking minority member of the House Committee and the Judiciary stating:

> There is no question that the nature of competition in sports differs, not only in degree but in kind, from the normal economic competition for markets which characterizes every other industry in this country . . .

> The problems which have been raised by the sports industry spokesmen . . . should not be viewed as flimsy facades voiced in order to justify the status quo. While there is surely a hint of exaggeration in some of their declarations, at the core of their arguments are some very real problems which go to the special nature competition in the sports industry.

2 Antitrust—Its Intent and Application to Baseball

The relationship between professional sports and antitrust principles has been a subject of much economic interest and discussion over the years. Part of the interest arises because sports leagues present an interesting puzzle for economists, offering an unusual type of enterprise on which to test economic theories. Also, sports may have allowed some economists to combine business and pleasure. Surely it is more fun to analyze the economics of baseball or football than, say, pricing patterns in the cast-iron-pipe industry. More realistically, much of the interest probably stems from the extensive media coverage and public discussion of economic events in sports—players' contract negotiations, changes in ownership, creation of new franchises, new ticket prices, and so forth.

Most economic studies of professional sports in general, and of professional baseball in particular,[1] acknowledge the peculiar characteristics of clubs and leagues that distinguish them from typical business enterprises. Nonetheless, the authors usually have proceeded to analyze professional sports in terms of conventional microeconomic models. Hence, they have reached conclusions concerning public policy toward professional sports which fail to take these peculiarities into account.[2]

Historical Background

The history of baseball's immunity from the antitrust laws is quite well known and merits only passing attention. The first hint of baseball's favored status came in 1914 in *American League Baseball Club* v. *Chase,* when the special term of the Supreme Court of New York denied equitable enforcement of a player contract against Hal Chase, "the best first baseman in professional baseball."[3] The Court held that the contract, which incorporated the reserve system, lacked mutuality, was unconscionable, and was monopolistic in violation of New York common law. Nevertheless, it held that the contract was not subject to the Sherman Act because

> baseball is an amusement, a sport, a game that comes clearly within the civil and criminal law of the state, and it is not a commodity or an article of merchandise subject to the regulation of Congress on the theory that it is interstate commerce.[4]

7

The reasoning in the *Chase* dictum was affirmed by Justice Holmes in the landmark *Federal Baseball Club* v. *National League* case.[5] The plaintiff in *Federal Baseball Club* alleged violations of the Sherman and Clayton Acts on the part of the major leagues by means of their reserve system. Justice Holmes, relying on the commerce-clause construction in *Hooper* v. *California,* held that professional baseball was neither engaged in nor interfering with commerce among the states.[6] Therefore baseball was not subject to the Sherman or Clayton Act.

Developments since *Federal Baseball Club* have obviously struck at the fundamental basis for that decision. First, after 1914 Congress greatly expanded its powers relating to commerce, especially during the New Deal era beginning in the 1930s. In leading cases such as *Wickard* v. *Filburn,* the Supreme Court gave a broad reading of Congress's power to enact laws regulating commerce among the states.[7] There has evolved from this process a much more encompassing definition of commerce than that implied in *Federal Baseball Club.* Concurrently, baseball has progressively become more involved with, and dependent on, interstate broadcasting and telecasting. The pooled sale of national broadcasting rights accounts for roughly one-tenth of baseball's total revenues, and many individual clubs broadcast their games in multistate regions.

These developments notwithstanding, the Supreme Court has consistently held that the antitrust immunity granted to major-league baseball in *Federal Baseball Club* will stand unless and until Congress acts to overturn it. In *Toolson* v. *New York Yankees,*[8] the Supreme Court upheld *Federal Baseball Club* on the grounds that "Congress had no intention of including the business of baseball within the scope of the federal antitrust laws."[9] And again, in *Flood* v. *Kuhn* in 1972, the Court not only upheld baseball's federal antitrust immunity but also held the state antitrust laws of New York to be inapplicable, both because of the need for national uniformity in the regulation of major-league baseball clubs and because of the overriding federal policy of not subjecting baseball to antitrust prosecution.[10] As recently as *Finley* v. *Kuhn* (1977, *cert. denied*) the Court upheld baseball's antitrust immunity.

Considerations in addition to the *stare decisis* effect of *Federal Baseball Club* have influenced the Court in upholding the baseball immunity. In both *Toolson* and *Flood,* the Court emphasized that professional baseball as a business had made its many decisions for fifty years in reliance on its antitrust immunity. In *Flood* the Court explicitly stated its preference that any action removing or modifying this immunity be made prospectively by Congress. As the Second Circuit Court had noted in *Flood,*

Baseball's welfare and future should not be for politically insulated interpreters of technical antitrust statutes, but rather should be for the voters through their elected representatives. If baseball is to be damaged by statutory regulation, let the Congressman face his constituents the next November and also face the consequences of his baseball voting record.[11]

With Congress thus charged by the courts with this responsibility, the proper application of antitrust law to the business of professional sports has been the subject of continued legislative concern for over two decades. Among the subjects of congressional interest have been the player-allocation systems; league rules governing the sale, allocation, and movement of franchises; and terms governing the marketing of broadcasting rights. Aside from these particular practices, one subject has commanded special congressional scrutiny—the unique, judicially created, antitrust immunity of baseball.

In 1977, the House Select Committee on Professional Sports, chaired by Congressman Sisk, issued a lengthy report that primarily addressed these antitrust issues. Yet in spite of extensive hearings on the same topics, no issues were resolved, and the Sisk committee, like its predecessors, initiated no legislation to change baseball's antitrust status.

Congressional inaction in the face of a status quo it has found cause to question is best understood from the perspective of conflicting public policies. On the one hand, our national antitrust policy outlaws undue market power and collective action among ostensibly competing businesses. The existing situation in baseball is in apparent conflict with these time-honored antitrust principles because of the variety of concerted leaguewide and industrywide actions that characterize the game and sports business practices generally. On the other hand, national values call for upholding the playing of professional sports as traditionally exercised, as well as preserving the singular quality of sports as an industry. The league structure, and the cooperative action it demands, is one of the elements of baseball that its adherents seek to preserve. Another is the stability of clubs and club rosters. Their continuation necessitates protection from the unrestricted entry and exit of clubs, as well as protection from complete player mobility that is a feature of unfettered competition. These components of the sports industry also reflect its uniqueness as an inherently cooperative enterprise. Clearly in many aspects, league sports do not automatically fit the competitive-market paradigm.

Antitrust Principles

The appropriate framework for assessing the welfare implications of the structure, conduct, and performance of industry derives in part from the theory of "ideal" output analysis as first developed by Professor Arthur C.

Pigou.[12] Under certain restrictive assumptions, it can be mathematically proved that the "ideal" output—that output which yields the highest total satisfaction to a society given its stock of resources—is obtained when the marginal social utility of each output in the economy is equated with its marginal social costs.[13] Under the assumption that they allocate their expenditures rationally, consumers will purchase each good in quantities such that its marginal utility is proportional to its price; and under conditions of perfect competition, each producer will produce up to the point that the marginal cost of each of its outputs is equal to its price as established by supply and demand in the marketplace. Accordingly, the "ideal" output is ensured if and only if all industries operate under conditions of perfect competition.[14]

In practice, this ideal output model serves as a starting point for assessing the welfare implications of the structure, conduct, and performance of industry. It rests on a set of simplifying assumptions that are not likely to be fulfilled in the "real" economic world,[15] and consequently the model's conclusions must be reassessed under more realistic assumptions. For example, the ideal output model pertains to a static state economy. When the dynamic aspects of the economic world in which we live are taken into account, the policy implications may change. In particular, the accepted notion that perfect competition best serves society does not hold if it can be shown that at least some degree of market power is essential to undertaking the risks of socially desirable innovations.[16]

Subject to these limitations, welfare economics nevertheless has provided an economic basis for a set of reasonably operational and generally accepted standards for assessing the structure, conduct, and performance of industry. The more important standards are as follows:

1. An appreciable number of sellers in each market, preferably as many as are consistent with scale economies
2. The absence of artificial barriers to entry
3. No collusion among producers on price, output, or sales
4. Evidence of vigorous rivalry among competing sellers in terms of their response to opportunities for profitable expansion, product improvement, and cost-reducing techniques
5. The absence of abnormally high profits that cannot be explained in terms of superior performance
6. A sufficiently high degree of knowledge on the part of consumers to permit them to exercise rational choice[17]

While no one would claim that these standards would be uniformly interpreted and applied by all analysts to any given industry, they reflect, at least in broad terms, our national policy toward private industry as expressed in our body of antitrust laws. For example, section 1 of the Sherman Act makes unlawful any contracts, combinations, and conspiracies that restrain trade or commerce. (Violations in the original act were misdemeanors; since 1974 they have been felonies.) Section 2 of the Sherman Act makes it unlawful to monopolize, attempt to monopolize, or combine or conspire with another person to monopolize.

While certain exceptions may be noted, section 1 is generally applicable to two or more parties, and contractual arrangements or agreements (tacit or overt) between or among them that restrain their independent actions are declared per se unlawful. That is, such agreements as those fixing prices, dividing territorial markets, boycotting suppliers or customers, or tying in products are in and of themselves violative of the Sherman Act, and defendants cannot offer the defense that such agreements are *reasonable* restraints. Section 2, on the other hand, generally is adjudicated under a "rule of reason." That is, in determining whether conduct is "monopolizing," courts have been inclined to undertake a more judgmental consideration of the alleged situation and the context in which it occurred.

Section 7 of the Clayton Act (the statute governing business mergers) is designed to prevent market concentration and the elimination of competitors by outlawing the acquisition of the stock or assets of one corporation by another corporation where the "effect . . . may be substantially to lessen competition or to tend to create a monopoly" in any line of commerce in any section of the country. Other antitrust statutes include Section 2 of the Clayton Act (as amended by the Robinson-Patman Act), which outlaws price discrimination, and section 5 of the Federal Trade Commission Act, which outlaws unfair methods of competition. The Wheeler-Lea amendment to the FTC Act prohibits deception and misrepresentation, especially in the advertising and promotion of consumer goods.

The essential purposes of the foregoing statutes that constitute the nation's antitrust policy are reasonably clear. In their application to business enterprise, they seek to foster open and free competition for consumer patronage among competing firms by making available to the buying public a wide range of choice as to source of supply, price, and product variety. This objective is perceived to be best served when the number of independent sellers in the relevant market is reasonably large, with each seller seeking to maximize its profits through independent actions, constrained not by agreements, arrangements, and agreed-upon rules but only by the impartial and impersonal forces of the marketplace. It is this latter requirement that is controlling. In practice, the ideal of a large number of "atomistic" sellers often is not met because of economies of scale. Yet even in industries that have become relatively concentrated, such as steel, tires, automobiles, and many others, firms may continue to hold large market shares as long as they avoid the particular proscriptions of antitrust laws.

The essential requirements are that they pursue their objective independently of their rivals and that they avoid commercial practices which the courts have tended to construe as monopolizing or attempts to monopolize.

Antitrust Issues and Baseball

Three institutional arrangements that govern the conduct of major-league baseball have led some analysts of professional sports to conclude that baseball functions as a cartel, one that would violate the antitrust laws if it were found to exist in other industries.[18] These arrangements are (1) the control over entry of new franchises into the league; (2) the territorial exclusivity that goes with a league franchise; and (3) player-control arrangements (the reserve system). Indeed, collective control over such factors as entry, the geographical market, and competition for an essential factor of production historically has been among the preoccupations of cartelized industries. But to conclude uncritically from this that major-league baseball functions as a conventional cartel ignores both the motivational forces behind cartel formation and the peculiar features of league sports.

Formal cartels have been defined as "compacts providing administrative machinery for regulating output, sharing markets, and fixing prices."[19] These are interdependent activities directed toward the avoidance of price competition among otherwise competing rival firms, and through output limitations they raise the uniform price among such firms above the competitive level. Such cartel arrangements have generally been found in commodity-type industries producing such standardized outputs as sugar, rubber, nitrogen, aluminum, magnesium, basic chemicals, and, allegedly, oil.[20] Typically, each individual cartel member can independently increase its output at relatively low additional costs. The objective of the cartel is to ensure that such individual action, which is motivated by the desire of gaining business at the expense of the rest of the industry and results in making all members of the industry worse off, does not occur.

In many aspects of the business, particularly in the sale of games, it is easy to detect fundamental distinctions between I.G. Farben, for example, the once-prominent member of the international chemical cartel, and, say, the Boston Red Sox, a member of the American League. Unlike in the situation of a typical cartel member, no league regulations restrict the Red Sox organization in the level and mix of admission prices, the contractual ties it negotiates with the media in locally broadcasting or telecasting its games, its parking fees, concession prices, or the financial terms it works out in player trades with other clubs.[21] Nor in any practical sense can it be said that the Red Sox club limits its output for the good of the total league membership—the 162-game season offers many more games than the other major sports do and covers virtually every day of the season on which the Boston weather permits sensible fans (and players) to occupy Fenway Park.

On the *input* side of the business, the market for players, the similarity to a cartel is much more apparent. By collective agreement among clubs composing a major league, each club is (1) limited to an active team roster of twenty-five players and a total of forty players under contract; (2) bound by the league schedule and the rules under which games will be played; (3) party to the major-league rules governing the free-agent draft; and (4) party to the collective-bargaining agreement with the Major League Baseball Players Association, which among other things governs the operation of the reserve system.

Also, in terms of entry, each club is empowered to vote on the admission of new clubs into the leagues and unilaterally to exercise its territorial exclusivity.

These agreements certainly give the *appearance* of collusive arrangements designed to restrict the employment of players and to keep their salaries below a competitive price. (That appearance was, of course, much stronger before the advent of free agents and multimillion-dollar contracts.) Another factor that contributes to the appearance of a cartel is the secrecy surrounding clubs' profits. Practically all clubs are privately held corporations (although a few are partnerships), and generally they have been unwilling to discuss their finances in public.[22] As a result, the rumors and speculations about club profits—by the press, by players, and even by other club owners—have been a colorful sideshow of the sport. The speculations often hint at enormous "monopoly profits."

With respect to the antitrust issues summarized above, the remainder of this book focuses on the following types of questions:

1. Are there alternatives to the cartel explanation for these agreements?
2. What are the structure and dynamics of baseball as it has evolved with these league agreements in place?
3. What, in fact, are the profits of baseball clubs?
4. What are the identifiable anticompetitive effects of these agreements?
5. If such agreements were outlawed, what would be the effect on baseball?

Given the controversial nature of the subject, it will never be possible to answer these questions to everyone's satisfaction. However, an examination of baseball with these questions in mind can add some sense of order to the confusion and controversy that have surrounded the sport.

In chapter 3 we discuss several inherent characteristics of baseball (and of league sports in general) that distinguish it from many other types of businesses. These characteristics affect the applicability of the analytical tools of microeconomic theory in general, and of antitrust principles in particular, to baseball as an industry.

Notes

1. Cf. Roger N. Noll, ed., *Government and the Sports Business* (Washington: The Brookings Institution, 1974); G. Ross, *Essays on the Economics of the Professional Team Sports Industry* (Ann Arbor, Mich.: University Microfilms International, 1974); and Daniel J. Gallagher, "An Economic Analysis of the Player Reservation System in Professional Team Sport Industry in the United States" (Ph.D. diss., University of Maryland, 1976).

2. An exception to this general assumption in regard to analysis of the reserve system in player contracts may be found in Gallagher, ibid., especially chapter 2.

3. 149 N.Y.S. 6 (1914).

4. 149 N.Y.S. 6, 17 (1914).

5. 259 U.S. 200 (1922).

6. 155 U.S. 648 (1895).

7. 317 U.S. 111 (1942).

8. 346 U.S. 356 (1953).

9. 346 U.S. 356, 357.

10. 407 U.S. 258 (1972).

11. 443 F.2nd 264, quoted in 407 U.S. 258, 268 (1972).

12. Arthur C. Pigou, *The Economics of Welfare,* 4th ed. (New York: Macmillan Co., 1929), especially pt. 2. Pigou built on the earlier theory of Vilfredo Pareto, whose welfare model is referred to as the "Pareto-optimum" solution to resource allocation. (*Welfare economics* is a broad term referring to the study of equity and efficiency of an economic system.)

13. For a detailed exposition of this proposition, see J.W. Markham, *The American Economy* (New York: George Braziller, 1963), pp. 28-42.

14. This follows because if firms operate under conditions other than perfect competition—that is, they possess some degree of monopoly power—they produce to the point where marginal costs equal marginal revenues which, in such a situation, are not equal to price. Hence, in the presence of monopoly, the marginal costs of all outputs are not equated with their respective marginal utilities (prices).

15. The most important are: (1) private and social costs are equal; (2) society's income is uniquely distributed; and (3) neither society's preferences nor production costs are affected by the structure of industry. See Markham, *The American Economy,* p. 32.

16. For an excellent reference on this issue, see Frederick M. Scherer, *Industrial Market Structure and Economic Performance* (Chicago: Rand McNally & Co., 1970), chapter 15.

17. Cf. Stephen H. Sosnick, "A Critique of Concepts of Workable Competition," *Quarterly Journal of Economics,* August 1958, pp. 380-423. A similar set of standards is developed in Scherer, ibid., chapter 2.

18. Cf. Henry G. Demmert, *The Economics of Professional League Sports* (Lexington, Mass.: Lexington Books, D.C. Heath and Co., 1974). "Of major import, however, are joint activities dealing with the economic aspects of firm interdependencies—those collective decisions which in effect make the industry a cartel, which would certainly be violative of antitrust statutes were they to occur in other types of enterprise" (p. 16). See also Noll, *Government and the Sports Business*, p. 2.

19. George W. Stocking and Myron Watkins, *Cartels in Action* (New York: Twentieth Century Fund, 1946), p. 3.

20. Ibid., p. 14.

21. Under his "best interests of baseball" powers, the commissioner of baseball at times has blocked trades or insisted on noncash compensation (for example, draft picks) in player trades. The commissioner's stated intent is to reduce the chance of "rich" clubs buying all the best talent.

22. Over the years, only a handful of clubs have released their annual financial statements to the public. For example, the Baltimore Orioles did so for many years, the Chicago Cubs do so currently.

3 Distinctive Characteristics of Baseball as an Economic Enterprise

Professional baseball is a league sport. It is important to recognize that leagues have a number of characteristics that, at least on the surface, appear to be inherently in conflict with antitrust principles of economics. By their very nature, leagues require a high degree of cooperation among their members. Leagues also possess unusual internal dynamics that affect the behavior of their members.

The concept of a league sport has roots going back at least as far as ancient Greece, when games were staged with athletes from many cities who played according to a common set of rules of competition. A league structure in any sport, whether it be bowling or baseball, offers several attractions:

1. *A discipline which, in itself, heightens interest and stimulates the athletes.* League rules provide athletes with a uniform basis of comparison. By standardizing the rules of play, a league fosters competition among a wide group of contestants from different places or even at different times. Records that are established become benchmarks for succeeding generations of players to try to surpass. Pete Rose's effort in 1978 to beat Joe DiMaggio's record number of hits in consecutive games, and the excitement surrounding his attempt, would have been meaningless without consistent rules and standards of play.

2. *A higher quality of play.* With a wider group of contestants, it is more likely that strong athletes will have an opportunity to play others of similar strength and thus be pushed to higher levels of exertion. Being best in the world is more meaningful than being best in the United States or best in Philadelphia.

3. *A structure for matching contestants of equal ability.* Contests are most exciting when the outcome is uncertain. League organizations in many sports group themselves in such a way as to prevent lopsided contests, such as happens, for example, when college football teams line up their opponents often several years in advance. Evenly matched games are more likely to stimulate their participants to higher levels of effort and ingenuity. Besides raising spectator interest, close, hard-fought contests help promote further development of the art.

4. *A structure for organizing individual contests into a meaningful season or a race.* Interest and the sense of drama are greatly heightened when

contestants play a series of games that culminate in a championship. Fans appear to feel that such a series provides a truer test of contestants' skill, strength and stamina than would a collection of randomly scheduled games.

In baseball, leagues developed spontaneously among the early amateur clubs during the 1850s. The first professional clubs, which were organized in 1869, were barnstormers, playing both amateurs and other professionals, wherever they could attract an opponent. By 1871, however, the clubs adopted a league structure to heighten spectator interest.

Inherent Tensions of a League Sport

A sports league, like many organizations, has a number of built-in tensions that arise because of conflicts between the interests of different members. One example is the need for enforcing rules and applying sanctions against disobedient members.

A key tension—one that occurs to some extent in all leagues and is particularly important in professional sports leagues—is the tradeoff between competitive balance and individual incentive. It is generally recognized that competitive balance among league members heightens the interest of spectators and spurs the athletes to exert themselves. However, contestants must feel that the rewards of winning are worth the effort. In most amateur sports, the personal drives of competition and accomplishment and the honor of winning are reward enough. For example, contestants train for years in the hope of becoming even an Olympic finalist, if not a medal winner. In other sports, such as racing or golf, a monetary prize plays an important role in spurring on the contestants, although here again the honor of being champion adds to their motivation.[1]

Leagues use many mechanisms to promote equality of contestants or contesting teams. Examples include limits on number of team members, size and weight restrictions (for example, in boxing), equipment limitations (as in yacht racing), limits on coaching staffs (as in National Collegiate Athletic Association (NCAA) football), reverse-order drafts of new players, and so on. A few sports organizations also try to achieve balance in the scheduling of contests. For example, English soccer teams move up and down among the four divisions on the basis of their previous year's won-lost record.

Mechanisms to spur contestants to winning include prize money, medals, ribbons, pennants, titles, special privileges, rings, and so on. In professional league sports, such as baseball, there usually is no prize money as such during the regular season, but the pennant winners are rewarded by revenues that come from increased attendance.[2]

Figure 3-1 illustrates some of the major mechanisms currently used by major-league baseball to maintain the balance between the equality of teams' strengths and the rewards to individual clubs for winning. This structure has evolved over the past hundred years, and each item on the list has its own history of development. For example, later we show that teams' spending for players' salaries has become much more unequal since the 1976 collective-bargaining agreement was signed. If salaries are related to players' skills, as they appear to be, then the strength of teams may, as a consequence, become less balanced. It is quite possible that new mechanisms will be needed to realign this balance. (We discuss salaries further in chapter 4.)

This inherent tension—between equality of teams' strengths and rewards for winning—is a recurring theme in the chapters that follow. A recognition of this tension is important in understanding the behavior of baseball clubs.

Distinctive Features of Major League Baseball as a Business

First, the "product" of baseball—the game—necessitates *cooperative rather than independent action*. Unlike industrial firms a baseball club generally cannot produce without the cooperation of its rivals. In baseball, as in ballroom dancing, it takes two to tango in order to produce a game. For this reason the game is sometimes described by economists as an "inverted joint product."[3]

An individual game requires that the contesting clubs agree on the time and place, rules, and distribution of revenues. The degree of necessary cooperation becomes enormous when the product is expanded to include a baseball season for a league consisting of many teams. For the major leagues to function, all members must agree on a schedule, the home-away split of gate receipts, broadcast arrangements and the division of broadcasting revenues, and, among others, divisional play-offs and World Series arrangements.

This requirement for cooperation immediately places baseball in apparent conflict with antitrust principles. In most businesses it would not be desirable for all firms to agree to produce equal quantities of a standardized product or to agree in advance on how to divide the revenues among themselves. Yet, in baseball, "production" of a season *requires* that these matters be determined by negotiation among the producers. Such types of agreements are reasonable means for improving the product, and without them the product, as we know it, could not exist.

Courts and Congress have recognized the need for special, seemingly collusive, agreements among league sports teams which deal with such

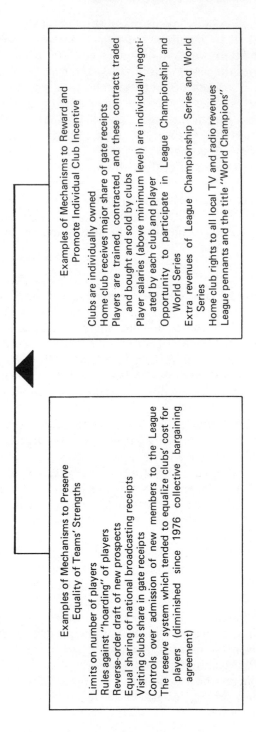

Figure 3-1. Major-League Baseball: How Balance Is Maintained between Equality of Team Strengths and Rewards for Winning

Examples of Mechanisms to Preserve Equality of Teams' Strengths

Limits on number of players
Rules against "hoarding" of players
Reverse-order draft of new prospects
Equal sharing of national broadcasting receipts
Visiting clubs share in gate receipts
Controls over admission of new members to the League
The reserve system which tended to equalize clubs' cost for players (diminished since 1976 collective bargaining agreement)

Examples of Mechanisms to Reward and Promote Individual Club Incentive

Clubs are individually owned
Home club receives major share of gate receipts
Players are trained, contracted, and these contracts traded and bought and sold by clubs
Player salaries (above minimum level) are individually negotiated by each club and player
Opportunity to participate in League Championship and World Series
Extra revenues of League Championship Series and World Series
Home club rights to all local TV and radio revenues
League pennants and the title "World Champions"

issues. An example is the special legislation that permits joint sales of national television rights and thus eliminates competition by individual teams for such sales. Another example is the legislation that was passed to permit the merger of the National and American Football Leagues.

Second, *the quality of baseball as a product is not independently determined by individual clubs.* A given automobile manufacturer may produce fine cars even if all its rivals produce "lemons." But in baseball even a star-studded team cannot consistently produce a good game against a team of cast-off scrubs. This is another way of stating that the commercial success of any one club is very much dependent on that of other clubs composing the league. While the prospect that the home team will slaughter the visiting club may be an added inducement to a small contingent of home-team fans, studies have shown that professional baseball attendance is positively affected by (among other factors) (1) uncertainty of the game's outcome, (2) closeness of the pennant race, and (3) number of star players on the two competing teams.[4]

The interdependence of commercial success among clubs constituting a league and the importance of league balance are fundamental characteristics that distinguish baseball clubs from conventional businesses.[5] For example, it would not be in any one club's interest to consistently hold a decisive competitive advantage over all other clubs in the league. In fact, such a situation eventually could have devastating consequences for the league itself. Consider, for example, a hypothetical situation where (1) the Cincinnati Reds won the National League pennant every year for eight years; (2) in each year the second-place team ended the season ten games out of first place; and (3) baseball fans in all National League cities fully expected Cincinnati to win the pennant. According to the studies cited above, attendance at Cincinnati's own games (to say nothing of that of other teams in the league) would reasonably be expected to be substantially less than if the pennant race were close and fans foresaw a reasonable chance that Cincinnati might be knocked out of first place.

This interdependence of clubs with regard to team strength means that it is in their long-term economic interest to maintain a reasonably competitive balance on the playing field. In the long run, the clubs have recognized this fact and have adopted balancing measures, such as the reverse-order draft of new prospects. However, there is an ebb and flow between a club's recognition of long-run and short-run interests. Balancing measures tend to occur at irregular intervals—often several years apart—and in response to a crisis or a reform movement. In the interim, in the heat of day-to-day competition, individual clubs frequently try to find loopholes or ways to get around the rules, in the hope of gaining an edge over their opponents.[6]

Agreements aimed at achieving competitive balance—principally the reserve system—have been the greatest source of lawsuits and antitrust controversy surrounding baseball and other league sports.[7] It is not hard to understand why. Most of the rules that have been devised to regulate teams' strengths have, in the final analysis, limited their use of *inputs* in the form of players, equipment, facilities, and so on. Any such limitation on inputs will inevitably reduce the market for the sellers of that input by reducing either the quantity purchased or the price teams pay. Thus it is not surprising that most of the antitrust lawsuits have been initiated by the sellers of inputs (mostly players).

Other types of rules that might be used to equalize teams' strengths are ones that reduce the reward or incentive for winning. An example might be a more equal division of gate revenues. We discussed this possiblity with a number of major-league owners, and they generally opposed the idea. One of them summed it up this way: "Several clubs in this league are not pulling their weight in promoting baseball in their communities. Why should I subsidize their poor attendance?"[8]

Third, *a league could not exist under unconstrained freedom of entry.* It is obvious from the lead time required for the scheduling of games, the accompanying complicated team logistics, and the interdependence of team activities that a league could not accommodate one of the essential features of a competitive market required of industries generally, namely, freedom of entry.[9] Since a club cannot produce games without the cooperation of other clubs, a potential entrant does not bear the full cost of entry into a league; the addition of a new franchise affects the costs and revenues of all other clubs in the league.

In some circumstances a new entrant can also impose a direct economic cost on the existing league members. Since the length of the season is fixed, the creation of new franchises reduces the number of games that a club can play with the older, recognized clubs that tend to draw more fans. The admission of Seattle and Toronto as expansion clubs to the American League in 1977 meant that such established teams as Boston, Chicago, Detroit, Baltimore, New York, and Cleveland played fewer games among themselves. Games among these older clubs generally attract higher attendance than do games with expansion clubs. For example, when Boston played three home games with Seattle, a new member of the league, in early May of 1977, the average attendance per game was only 11,000. In the preceding week, a three-game series with Detroit in Boston drew an average attendance of about 30,000—in spite of colder weather and the fact that one of the games was a midweek day game.[10] If baseball functioned purely as a cartel, it would constantly limit its membership to those teams that could maximize total attendance throughout the season. Not only might the leagues refuse to admit most expansion clubs, but also they would seek to eliminate those existing franchises with low attendance in order to increase the number of games among high-attendance clubs.

The success of expansion franchises in most professional sports, especially basketball and hockey, has been rather mixed. At least on the surface, expansion would appear to be a risky strategy for an established league. Why, then, do leagues expand? Part of the answer, we believe, lies in the threat of "league wars."

One way to achieve "entry" into a league sport, if the established league is unwilling to expand, is to start a new league. This strategy was tried a number of times during the early history of baseball, and more recently new leagues have appeared increasingly in other professional sports. Some of these leagues (for example, the American Football League or the American Basketball Association) have been relatively successful. Thus, the threat of potential new leagues serves as a check on existing leagues that fail to recognize new market opportunities.

It is not at all clear that freedom of entry would result in many new major-league clubs. We analyze and discuss in chapter 4 some of the factors that determine market potential for baseball clubs. Our results appear to agree with earlier studies by others who took a slightly different perspective.[11] Basically, these studies concluded that as of 1975, a club needed to sell approximately 1 million to 1.25 million seats per year in order to survive, and to achieve such an attendance ordinarily requires a metropolitan population of substantially more than 1 million. We are speaking here of averages. Some clubs in smaller metropolitan areas (for example, Cincinnati) have prospered by playing very good baseball or by drawing fans from greater than normal distances. Similarly, some clubs in much larger markets have drawn poor attendance (for example, Oakland, California, and Washington, D.C.). Several of the present clubs are in cities that appear to be of a borderline size, such as Kansas City, Milwaukee, San Diego, and Seattle. In these cases the success of franchises will depend strongly on team performance and the aggressive promotion of baseball.

There have been occasional suggestions that some large metropolitan areas, particularly New York, could support more teams than they now do. However, the past record of multiple-team markets, in baseball or in other sports, has not been encouraging in this regard. A new team in, say, Newark, New Jersey, would probably run as much as or more risk of failure than a new one in a much smaller market without a nearby competitor. In any event, it would appear that the major-league expansion from sixteen to twenty-six clubs between 1960 and the present has been broadly consistent with the growth of market opportunities.

Baseball clubs are not in competition with one another for customers. While clubs constituting a league compete with one another for league standing, they do not, because of the geographical nature of the "market," compete for customers. Except possibly for an insignificant contingent of itinerant fans, the attendance at a Baltimore-Boston game is unaffected by the attendance on the same day at a game between Detroit and Cleveland.

This is not meant to imply that absolutely no competition for customers exists among major-league clubs. The four large metropolitan areas supporting two or more clubs may be characterized by a certain amount of interclub competition for patronage and fan loyalty. Moreover, the network telecast of a major-league game may compete with a hometown game played on the same day. The essential point, however, is that such fringe competition is not likely to affect the decision making of individual clubs in such matters as ticket prices. Thus, ticket prices are likely to be determined not by competition with other clubs but by competition with alternate uses of people's leisure time, such as television, going to the beach, or puttering around the yard. The revenues earned by a club for any given home game are determined much more by its own league standing and its relative standing with the visiting team than by any independent competitive commercial strategy it may adopt against other teams in its league. Even if it reduces its admission prices for home games, the Boston Red Sox organization will not substantially affect the attendance at Wrigley Field in Chicago. In economic terms, the price cross-elasticity of demand among games played in different home ball parks is extremely low—in fact, in most cases it is virtually zero.[12]

The absence of direct competition with other baseball clubs does not reduce the need for marketing and promotion activities. Baseball parks, especially for clubs not in contention for the pennant, are seldom filled to capacity, so that clubs have a direct incentive to attract more people to their games. Increasingly in recent years, other spectator sports and leisure activities have competed for fans' attention. Professional sports teams seem to have recognized this factor of late and are recruiting sales and marketing managers (from outside the sports industry) to apply up-to-date concepts and marketing techniques.

Fifth, *baseball clubs do not appear to conform to the conventional profit-maximization model used to analyze other businesses.* As stated earlier, while analysts may recognize the peculiarities of major-league sports that distinguish them from other business enterprises, most have proceeded as though these distinctions did not exist. Particularly, most previous studies have assumed that the goal of maximizing profits, generally assumed to be the goal of business firms, offered a satisfactory explanatory hypothesis for the conduct and performance of baseball clubs. The essential features of profit-maximizing assumptions are that in the short run, firms will maximize profits (or minimize losses) on their precommitted capital investment by setting prices and the rate of output so that their marginal costs equal marginal revenues, and that in the long run, they will allocate capital to industries that offer the highest prospective rate of return, with due consideration for risks. Economist Michael Canes, applying this profit-maximization model to baseball, has argued that a club owner would spend more to increase the quality of the team until the additional revenue generated at home and away, because of the last increment in quality, would exactly equal the costs of the quality increase. And Noll, although his statistical results showed that baseball clubs did *not* price their admission tickets at the profit-maximizing level, nevertheless concluded that profit maximizing by baseball clubs could not be rejected out of hand.[13]

Baseball clubs, however, exhibit a number of characteristics that suggest that their primary goals are something more than just profits. Examples include the willingness of some clubs to sustain operating losses for many years in succession, support to failing clubs, and, until the cost pressures of the late 1970s, a seeming inattention of many clubs to marketing and full exploitation of their market opportunities. The next section develops these hypotheses further.

Nonfinancial Motivations

So far we have dealt with baseball clubs as *economic* enterprises. It would be unrealistic to overlook the *noneconomic* aspects of owning and running baseball clubs. Baseball cannot be understood without recognizing that most owners are wealthy individuals who have already made their fortunes in some other career before buying into baseball. Examples include Ray Kroc, the builder of the McDonalds' hamburger chain, who owns the San Diego Padres; the Wrigley family, from the chewing gum company of the same name, who owns a controlling interest in the Chicago Cubs; George Steinbrenner, who, having amassed a fortune in the American Shipbuilding Co., acquired a major interest in the New York Yankees; and so on.

These are people who have plenty of attractive business opportunities for investment. Yet there are popular stories of owners who for years and years have subsidized ball clubs that have lost money. Tom Yawkey supported the Boston Red Sox for thirty years before the team became successful. The Wrigleys and their Chicago Cubs have not seen a pennant since 1945. In any ordinary type of business enterprise, such owners would have liquidated or sold or moved the business long before thirty years had elapsed. Clearly there must be some motivation other than profit maximization for their continued support.

Economic theory provides one explanation in the form of "satisficing," a concept introduced about twenty years ago by Herbert Simon. Simon asserts that businessmen set profit goals for themselves which are not the *optimum* but are merely "good enough." Many companies could, by exerting themselves to the very limits of their capabilities, earn higher profits than they do. But, Simon argues, they "satisfice"—that is, they accept a somewhat lower level of profits that is sufficient to keep stockholders reasonably satisfied. The level of profits that is "good enough" will be a subjective judgment that depends on many factors, including the stockholders' other opportunities, their standard of living, and their personal values. For many baseball owners, a "good enough" level of financial performance appears to be at or near breakeven.

It would be naive to argue that baseball owners do not want to make profits when they can. On the other hand, a number of them do say that maximum profits are not the *primary* objective.

In preparing this book, we held lengthy conferences with ten American and National League club owners and with other club officials such as general managers. We also met with several owners and officials of the minor leagues. The objective of this field research was to ascertain the extent to which, and in what specific ways, major-league baseball clubs can be analyzed in terms of the same criteria employed in analyzing conventional business enterprises. Particularly, we sought to identify the extent to which those who own and manage clubs are governed by the commercial incentives that we assume motivate business enterprise generally in respect to pricing, decisions to enter or exit from an industry, response to profit incentives, product or service quality, employee relations, methods of finance, and other modes of business conduct and performance.

The evidence developed in the course of these field studies, while not of the hard variety, strongly suggests that baseball clubs do not comport with the traditional economic models of firm behavior usually applied to normal business enterprises. Primarily, this essential conclusion appears to follow directly from the fact that the majority of the ownership interests we studied were motivated to enter the baseball industry more out of reason of personal gratification, love of the game, devotion to professional sports generally, or out of civic pride than by the prospects of profits. But this conclusion also follows from the critical fact that the inherent nature of major-league baseball virtually precludes the possibility of clubs competing with one another in the conventional commercial sense.

Major-league baseball has generated considerable public discussion concerning the precise nature of its constituent organizations. The central issue in this regard has been whether a baseball club, as one of these organizations, is an "ordinary" business, organized and operated in much the same fashion as other profit-seeking businesses, such as automobile manufacturers, or is more akin to such quasi-civic or professional institutions as local chambers of commerce, Better Business Bureaus, the Boston Pops, or the National Gallery of Art.

Public discussion, while substantial, has not satisfactorily resolved the issue. Those who concentrate on the game itself—its history, its traditions, and its drama—are likely to perceive those who organize and manage it as nothing less than custodians of the very best aspects of Americana. George Grella, writing in the *Massachusetts Review* in 1975, described baseball as instructive, as beautiful, and as profound as the most significant aspects of American culture. It should be compared not only with other sports, but with our other indigenous arts—our painting, music, dance, and literature. In its theory and practice baseball embodies some of the central preoccupations of the cultural fantasy we like to think of as the American Dream.[14]

But even those who view it from its more commercial side sharply distinguish a baseball club from business generally. Leonard Koppett, a sportswriter and former member of the sports staff of *The New York Times,* has observed that

[Baseball] club owners are not ordinary businessmen.

To begin with, profit in itself is not the owner's primary motive. Any man with the resources to acquire a major league team can find ways to make better dollar-for-dollar investments. His payoff is in terms of social prestige—although it is nevertheless true that his other businesses may collectively profit from that prestige. A man who runs a $100-million-a-year business is usually anonymous to the general public; a man who owns even a piece of a ball club that grosses $5-million a year is a celebrity. His picture and comments are repeatedly published in newspapers known in every corner of his community. . . .

That does not mean, of course, that ball clubs don't seek profits . . . but the driving force is to be identified with a popular and successful team . . . and that motivation leads to important variations from "normal" business behavior.[15]

The field study of club owners produced factual evidence that is generally supportive of Koppett's overall assessment of major-league baseball as a business. The Milwaukee Brewers, a relatively new franchise in the American League, was one of the clubs covered. Since the former Milwaukee Braves had moved to Atlanta for financial reasons (according to all the information made public at the time), we were especially interested in the motives, the incentives, and the means of financing the new franchise.

According to Allen H. ("Bud") Selig, he and a group of interested citizens founded Teams Incorporated, a nonprofit enterprise, for the purpose of returning major-league baseball to Milwaukee. The search for a franchise took five years. After their application to both the American and National Leagues for an expansion club failed, Teams Incorporated sponsored ten of the Chicago White Sox home games as a preliminary step to buying the club and moving it to Milwaukee. Their offer to buy was refused. Finally, at the end of their five-year search, they purchased the Seattle club out of bankruptcy for $10.8 million, slightly over half of which ($5.8 million) was financed by the equity interests of "Bud" Selig and his associates, and the rest was financed by bank loans. Shortly afterward, the equity interest had to be increased by $3.3 million. While the source of the equity is not known in detail, the organizers obtained some of it by borrowing. According to Selig, the first three-year period, 1970 to 1972, when annual paid attendance ranged between 600,000 and 993,000, was very tough-going financially, but the club was helped considerably by the favorable stadium contract worked out with the County of Milwaukee. The contract provided that the club was to pay rent of $1.00 per patron, until attendance reached one million, and an increasing percentage of attendance revenue and 10 percent of concessions revenues thereafter. Parking revenues went to the stadium and those from concessions went to the club. The club paid all operating costs for baseball use. Even with the favorable stadium contract, the Milwaukee Brewers sustained substantial losses in each of their first three years.

The prime movers behind the Brewers asserted that civic motivation and love of major-league baseball, rather than the prospects of profit, were what actually sustained their efforts to bring the franchise to Milwaukee—an assertion that would appear to be consistent with the financial history of the franchise. They also asserted that they could contemplate no circumstances, including the prospects of higher financial rewards, that would induce them to move the Brewers away from Milwaukee.

In the case of virtually every club covered in the field study, the ownership and managerial interests stressed "hometown" interest and devotion to major-league baseball as the primary reason for their involvement. John Fetzer owned the Detroit Tigers and for many years owned their stadium outright—along with six TV stations. The stadium is located in the central city; it is old, and improvement costs and maintenance have run high (including property taxes, they have amounted to approximately $0.5 million per year in recent years—exclusive of normal operating expenses). Until the Detroit Lions moved to a new football stadium, Fetzer recovered a portion of his stadium costs by renting to the Detroit Lions.

In spite of high stadium costs, Fetzer reported that he turned down an offer by a suburban community to build a new stadium for the Tigers because, as he put it, it would be the end of midtown Detroit. Urban flight had left the city heavily populated with blue-collar and low-income workers, who were predominantly black. While his records showed that white-collar suburbanites attended baseball games more frequently than central-city residents did, he maintained that keeping the Tigers in town was essential to the preservation of what was left of inner-city Detroit.

Fetzer devoted 75 percent of his time to baseball and considered it essentially a labor of love. The Detroit club had sustained average annual operating losses of upward of $0.5 million in the two recent years for which data were available, but it should be pointed out that these were years in which Detroit had been rebuilding its club and not in serious contention for the league championship.

The Philadelphia Phillies had been a Carpenter family-held corporation since 1944. Ruly Carpenter, the present owner-operator, was an avid sports fan, having played varsity football and baseball during his college years at Yale. He had no ownership interest in other sports and devoted his entire time to the Phillies' organization, including its farm system. He attended and took copious notes on the meetings of farm club managers and coaches, which are devoted to assessments of players in the farm system and their assignment to the farm club. He studied the daily game reports on all teams in the Phillies' system and had a close personal relationship with the players, most of whom addressed him on a first-name basis. One needs only to live several days in close company with Ruly to be convinced that the Phillies were not simply his business; they were his professional life. He viewed his club as a Philadelphia institution, and would never consider moving elsewhere. This was no idle claim to civic allegiance; when the Phillies moved into a new city stadium seven years ago, Ruly signed a contract to stay there thirty years.

But while civic motivation and complete dedication to baseball characterized Ruly Carpenter, the Phillies, more than most clubs included in our field study, used modern concepts and techniques of management, especially in marketing. Carpenter and William Giles, the vice president in charge of marketing, had analyzed the diversity of their fans and seriously attempted to match the supply of seats at various prices to market demand—from deluxe boxes to the bleachers. Management took periodic surveys to ascertain the bounds of their geographic market, and had attempted to analyze the cross-price elasticity of demand between live attendance and pay television for home games (the Phillies telecast twenty-nine homes games on pay television during the 1978 season). The club's expenditures in recent years on publicity and promotion exceeded those of most clubs, averaging from 6 to 7 percent of gross baseball revenues.

More importantly, through a carefully administered player-development program, the Phillies had greatly improved their won-lost record. For the long period of 1900 to 1970, the club compiled a won-lost record of 44.3 percent and ranked, on average, tenth out of the eleven National League teams that had at least thirteen years in the league during that seventy-one-year period. In the 1970s the Phillies were generally a contending team, reaching the National League divisional play-offs in 1976, 1977, and 1978. They also have been one of the top spenders in the major leagues for player salaries. In 1976 the paid attendance reached 2.2 million and, for the first time in the club's history, surpassed the maximum combined Phillies-Athletics attendance of nearly 2.1 million in 1950. As a result of good management, good players, an attractive and well-designed stadium in the fourth largest National League city, the departure of the Philadelphia Athletics in 1955, and an effective player-development system, the Phillies operated at a profit for most of the mid-1970s.

Throughout this period the Phillies were active bidders in the free-agent market, and they signed star players to some of the highest salaries in baseball. It is an open question whether the club's profits might have been higher if it had spent less for players. By mid-1979 there were signs that Carpenter's resolve was beginning to weaken, and he publicly questioned whether baseball could continue to afford the current high levels of player compensation.

The Baltimore Orioles are an exception to the widely held view that winning teams with star players in large metropolitan areas are profitable enterprises. The Orioles have compiled the best ten-year won-lost record of any team in the American League. In the five-year period from 1972 to 1976 they won the American League pennant twice, came in second twice, and ended the 1972 season in third place, but only five games behind Detroit, the eastern division champions. In spite of this enviable field record, the Oriole franchise has operated at a loss on its baseball operations in all the recent years for which its financial statements are available.

The Baltimore club confronts, to a larger extent than most clubs, those economic pressures that have begun to exert themselves on medium-sized industrial cities. The Orioles rent the antiqued city stadium in Baltimore's inner city, however, on relatively favorable terms. The inner-city population does not attend baseball games in proportion to its numbers. For these two reasons—the old stadium and low attendance in the inner city—the Orioles have pursued a low-admission-price policy; the club's average ticket price of $2.69 (as recently as 1976) was the lowest in the American League. Meanwhile, soaring player salaries have substantially raised the club's costs, and prospects are that these increases will continue.

By the standard of financial performance applied to business generally, the Baltimore Orioles would be judged to be a failing company. Yet they persisted in this condition for a far longer time than most businesses would tolerate. According to the "Media Guides" published by the club, the top management of the Orioles (Jerold Hoffberger and Zanvyl Krieger) until very recently were Baltimoreans who were prominent in local affairs and devotees of professional sports. Hoffberger, chairman of the board since 1965, was also chief executive officer of Carling National Breweries, Inc., in Baltimore. His local activities included board memberships on the Johns Hopkins and Sinai hospitals and the Greater Baltimore committees. Additionally, he was an ardent horseman and long-time breeder of thoroughbred horses. Krieger, Oriole treasurer and chairman of the executive committee, was among the prime movers in bringing the Oriole franchise to Baltimore. He also played a prominent role in reestablishing professional football in Baltimore in 1953, served as the Colts' vice president and director, and from 1962 to 1974 was board chairman of the Baltimore American Hockey League franchise, the Clippers. Prominent in Baltimore civic affairs, Krieger was given the Award of Merit from the city of Baltimore in 1970.

In 1979 the Orioles were purchased by a Washington lawyer, Edward Bennett Williams. Despite public statements to the contrary, speculation ran high that he would move the club to a new stadium midway between Washington and Baltimore or play some of the home games in Washington—or that he would try in some way to attract fans from Washington as well as from Baltimore.

Summary

Two key characteristics of baseball distinguish it from other types of economic enterprises:

1. The high degree of interdependence among members of any league sport. From this interdependence flows a *requirement* for many types of agreement among the members. Some of those agreements, particularly those directed toward maintaining equality of teams' strengths, will tend to have an anticompetitive appearance.
2. The nonfinancial motivations of persons who establish and run baseball clubs. These considerations lead to a willingness to sustain losses or low profits for longer than most businesses would tolerate. They also affect the pricing of tickets and lead perhaps to a tendency to overinvest in players.

In the next two chapters, we show some of the effects of baseball's special characteristics in practical terms of governance, player careers, and finances.

Notes

1. For many years the rewarding of prize money was used to divide amateur sports from professional sports. More recently, however, it has been recognized that the lines are much more blurred. Even the Olympics offers a monetary prize in the form of opportunities for lecture tours, advertising endorsements, and the like, which are available to winners in some of the more popular sports.

2. This reward does not always occur. The Baltimore Orioles during the early 1970s and the Oakland Athletics in 1973, 1974, and 1975 are examples of pennant-winning teams that did not draw a large attendance and consequently earned relatively small rewards for their success. (We are speaking here of regular season attendance. These teams did, of course, participate in the division of World Series revenues.)

3. A conventional "joint product" is one necessarily produced in conjunction with another product, for example, gasoline and residuals in refinery runs. In other words, two (or more) products are produced by the same action. Baseball is a type of inverse situation—*two* actions (participation by two teams) are needed to make *one* product.

4. See chapter 4 for the analysis of the Cambridge Research Institute (CRI). Also see Roger N. Noll, ed., *Government and Sports Business* (Washington: The Brookings Institution, 1974), pp. 120-130. Population of the home city, age of stadium, certain demographic factors, per capita income, and ticket prices also affect attendance.

5. For purposes of this analysis, commercial success is provisionally equated with maximizing attendance. The validity of this assumption would hold for most club revenue sources such as gate receipts, concession sales, broadcasting rights, parking fees, and the like. Clubs can also increase revenues by trading players or selling their contracts. The implications of this are taken up later.

6. A good example is the tendency of clubs to hoard good players in their farm systems. A team with, say, a good catcher might keep two or three other potential star catchers locked up in its farm system so that they would not be available to other teams. Over the years, by plugging loophole after loophole, baseball has developed an elaborate set of controls to ensure that good potential players are either brought up to the majors by their parent club or made available for use by other clubs. See the discussion of the "Rule 5 Draft" in chapter 4.

7. This is true not only of professional sports but also of amateur sports. The NCAA has twice been sued because of rules that limit the number of coaches a college football team could have. The NCAA's rules both times have been upheld by the courts. See Carl L. Reisner, "Tackling Intercollegiate Athletics: An Antitrust Analysis," *Yale Law Journal*, January 1978, p. 76.

8. The National Football League uses a 60-40 home-away split in gate revenues, the most equal division currently in use among major team sports. Football's situation is somewhat unique, though, because most of its games are sold out. Thus, a different gate split would not significantly alter the regular season revenues of each team.

Professional basketball and hockey have no sharing of gate revenues. In baseball the split is 80-20 in the American League and something closer to 90-10 (according to a cents-per-admission formula) in the National League.

9. The limitations on freedom of entry also apply to freedom of exit; that is, they also affect the costs and revenues of all other clubs that comprise the league.

10. Taken from attendance data provided by the Boston Red Sox office. Assuming revenues (including concessions) of about $5 per fan, Boston's "investment" in the Seattle club amounted to something like $285,000 (in forgone revenues) for this three-game series.

11. Henry G. Demmert, *The Economics of Professional League Sports* (Lexington, Mass.: Lexington Books, D.C. Heath & Co., 1974); Noll, *Government and Sports Business*, p. 130.

12. It appears that price competition does not occur to any great extent in multiteam cities. Ticket prices of such teams are not significantly different from prices charged by other teams.

13. Noll, *Government and Sports Business*, p. 125. Noll calculated that the demand for baseball was inelastic at prevailing ticket prices.

14. Reprinted in *Eastern Review*, April 1977, p. 39. Reprinted with permission of *Massachusetts Review*.

15. Leonard Koppett, "A Strange Business, Baseball," *The New York Times Magazine*, September 2, 1973, p. 11. © 1973 by The New York Times Company. Reprinted by permission. Despite this comment, at times Koppett has harshly criticized baseball owners for what he believes are financially exploitative tactics or statements.

4 Structure and Dynamics of Major-League Baseball

Earlier chapters have treated baseball on a general level and provided a conceptual framework for understanding it as a league sport and for relating it to antitrust principles. In this and the following chapter we turn to specifics to demonstrate how the concepts relate to the practical realities of the enterprise known as professional baseball.

Baseball does not have a single monolithic structure, nor is it simply a collection of twenty-six interdependent clubs. Rather, it is a complex interactive network of organizations. This network is centered on the twenty-six major-league clubs, but there are other actors involved whose interests and behavior must be considered in order to understand the workings of the whole system. In this chapter we present a brief description of the major entities that make up major-league baseball and discuss some of their interactions. This discussion is amplified by a presentation of the flow of funds through baseball. We also deal with some of the dynamics of developing and retaining players. Finally, we take up the factor that affects the success of the whole enterprise, namely, the market potential for baseball games.

The Structural Components

Professional baseball is made up of a number of individual components that are bound together by sets of agreements and contractual relationships. The following are some of the key entities.

Major-League Clubs

At the heart of major-league baseball are the twenty-six major-league clubs. Each of these operates as an independent economic unit in such matters as contracting for players, promoting games and selling tickets, arranging for the use of stadia and for other supporting services and facilities, and negotiating local broadcasting of games. Each joins with other clubs to stage championship games, establish common rules and playing schedules, and so on.

Most clubs are partnerships or privately held corporations. A few, such as the St. Louis Cardinals or the Atlanta Braves, are subunits of larger corporations. Although people often think of baseball as being big business, the clubs are relatively small by today's standards. In 1977 the great majority had revenues between $5 million and $10 million.

The business of baseball clubs is limited almost exclusively to their major-league activities. Few of the clubs are "vertically integrated." For example, only four own their own stadia, and only a few minor-league clubs are owned by major-league parents. Three clubs are "vertically integrated forward" in that they purchase television time for their games, which they in turn sell to advertisers.

The twenty-six major-league clubs are located in twenty-two metropolitan areas, as shown in table 4-1. Four metropolitan areas—New York, Chicago, Los Angeles, and San Francisco-Oakland—have two major-league clubs.

Each major-league team maintains an active roster of twenty-four or twenty-five players through most of the playing season. In addition, each club can maintain fifteen or sixteen players "on option" in the minor leagues who might see major-league service during some portion of the playing season, making a total of forty players on major-league contracts. Each club plays a schedule of 162 games during the regular season, 81 at home and 81 away.

Major-League Agreement

Collectively, the major-league club owners establish most of the regulations which govern the industry. The convenant which binds them is the Major League Agreement, to which are attached the Major League Rules. The rules detail all the procedures the clubs have agreed on, including the rules for signing, trading, and dealing with players.

Office of the Commissioner

Under the Major League Agreement, the owners elect a commissioner of baseball for a seven-year term. Originally created after the Chicago "Black" Sox scandal of 1919, the office of the commissioner's main function is to maintain the integrity of the sport. The commissioner acts as a spokesman for the industry, resolves disputes among clubs and other baseball entities, polices the industry and enforces the rules. He has broad powers to protect the best interests of the game. The commissioner also administers the Major Leagues Central Fund, under which he negotiates and receives the revenues from national broadcast contracts for major-league games. Through the Major Leagues Central Fund the clubs pay for all con-

Table 4-1
Structure of Major-League Baseball, 1978

National League	American League
Eastern Division	*Eastern Division*
Philadelphia Phillies	New York Yankees
Pittsburgh Pirates	Boston Red Sox
Chicago Cubs	Milwaukee Braves
Montreal Expos	Baltimore Orioles
St. Louis Cardinals	Detroit Tigers
New York Mets	Cleveland Indians
	Toronto Blue Jays
Western Division	*Western Division*
Los Angeles Dodgers	Kansas City Royals
Cincinnati Reds	California Angels
San Francisco Giants	Texas Rangers
San Diego Padres	Minnesota Twins
Houston Astros	Chicago White Sox
Atlanta Braves	Oakland Athletics
	Seattle Mariners

Note: The teams are listed in order of league standing at the end of the 1978 season.

tributions to the players' benefit trust and for a number of other activities sponsored on the clubs' behalf. About half of the Fund's revenues are passed on directly to the clubs in approximately equal shares.

The Leagues

Within the overall structure of major-league baseball, the teams are organized into two leagues each with its own president and administration: the American League with fourteen teams and the National League with twelve teams (as shown in table 4-1). Each league controls the allocation and movement of baseball franchises. In both leagues, it takes a three-fourths vote of the owners to authorize the movement of a franchise, but there are different rules concerning the approval of new franchises and the placement of clubs in nearby cities (see chapter 6).

In addition to authorizing franchises, the leagues develop the schedule of games, contract for umpires, and perform other administrative tasks. The leagues are financed through a small percentage share of clubs' ticket revenues, and receipts from World Series and league championship games.

The present two-league structure has its origins in a competitive struggle at the turn of the century. The National League established the first "permanent" professional league in 1876. Interest in baseball subsequently grew, and several efforts were made to start a second league. Most ended in failure. The American League was founded as the Western League in 1892, and by raiding the National League clubs for more and better players than other would-be entrants had, the American League was able to attract a reasonable following. The resulting escalation in players' salaries was financially ruinous for both sides, however, and by 1903 they joined forces. Each league maintained its separate identity and preserved a degree of independence in setting rules (a good current example is the use of designated hitters by the American League), allocating franchises, scheduling, and so on. Most important, they agreed not to raid each other for players.

This pattern of a new, competing league either failing or being merged into the existing structure has been repeated many times in professional sports. Examples of these "league wars" include associations that have failed (the Federal Baseball League and the World Football League) and two that have merged (the American Football League and the American Basketball Association). The primary reason for either merger or failure is almost always the same: In order to acquire talented players quickly, the new league must raid the existing league. There is no other supply, in the short run, of acceptable talent, and without such players the new league cannot gain sufficient public interest in its games. A bidding war ensues and players' salaries are pushed to levels that many teams cannot sustain. Sooner or later, some fail or are so weakened that they are willing to negotiate a merger—always including an agreement not to compete for players—with the other side.

Why, one might ask, are players' salaries in these wars pushed to such high, unsustainable levels? The answer appears to lie in the very selective nature of public interest in sports. Professional sports are, first and foremost, an entertainment. They thrive on excitement, drama, humor, and colorful, interesting personalities. Without these ingredients people lose interest and look elsewhere for their entertainment. Admittedly, a few die-hard fans seem to persevere for years in support of teams that lack these qualities. However, sports fans appear to be very selective in preferring to see the best teams perform. Thus it helps a new league to have at least a few name players from the outset, to attract attention and convince fans that the league intends to provide games of comparable quality to those already being offered.

As the new league plays its first few seasons, the quality of games is easily apparent. Indeed, it is widely commented on in the press. In order to show promise of exciting, top-quality (or first-class or big-league) games, it is essential to bring in a number of recognized players from the established league. The mere act of signing a star player lends both credibility and excitement to the new league.

On the defensive side, if their star players are lured away, teams in the established league face not only the loss of team quality but also the possible loss of fan loyalty, not to mention likely public criticism for being "cheap," timid, stupid, or callous. These latter concerns may strike a sensitive nerve, particularly in owners who have nonfinancial motivations.

Major League Player Relations Committee

The twenty-six major-league teams have joined to form the Major League Player Relations Committee, Inc. The board of directors of the Major League Player Relations Committee consists of the two league presidents and six elected representatives of club managements. A major function of the committee is to negotiate the national collective-bargaining agreement with the Major League Baseball Players Association. The Player Relations Committee also administers the collective bargaining agreement on behalf of the clubs, for example, representing management at arbitration proceedings and handling press relations. The committee also provides advice and counsel to clubs on such matters as day-to-day player relations and individual player contract negotiations.

Major League Baseball Players Association

The Major League Baseball Players Association (MLBPA) is the players' union, and it negotiates the basic agreement with the clubs. This agreement sets the terms of employment, benefits, and minimum salaries. Unlike many other unions, the MLBPA has not been directly involved in negotiating salaries above the minimum. These rates are negotiated individually by players, often with the help of an agent, and their clubs. This unusual arrangement highlights one of the unique economic characteristics of professional sports, namely that players (that is, "labor") are not easily interchangeable. Although steelworkers or bricklayers, for example, may differ in skill, they generally can be grouped for bargaining purposes into a few grades or levels of people with similar capabilities. In baseball this type of approach runs into difficulties. There is no practical equivalence between, say, a Reggie Jackson and a left-handed outfielder with ten years of experience. Many players, especially the stars, are unique, nonfungible resources. As individuals, they possess far more bargaining power than they could as union members. Their situation is, in many ways, similar to that of actors, singers, and other performing artists. And, not surprisingly, the union contract in baseball and other aspects of player contracts are similar to those found in the motion-picture industry.

The MLBPA is financed by dues collected from each major-league player at a rate of $3 for every day on which they play (roughly $500 per year). However, these dues are more than offset by revenues which the MLBPA receives from the licensing of "group rights" for such uses as the baseball cards sold with bubble gum. In recent years, these license fees have amounted to about $700,000 per year, so that, in effect, each player has received free union membership plus a small income from the MLBPA.

Minor Leagues

In addition to the major-league teams, there were 156 minor-league clubs in 1978 (see figure 4-1). These clubs were located throughout the United States, Canada, and Mexico. Minor-league teams serve a dual function: they are entertainment entities in their own right, and they serve as a training ground for major-league players.

Each major-league club owns or contracts with four to six minor-league clubs. (Figure 4-2 shows the thirty-eight-year trend in the number of minor-league clubs and their attendance.) This farm system ordinarily includes a team in each level: Rookie, class A, class AA, and class AAA. About twenty minor-league clubs are owned outright by major-league parents. The remainder are independent corporations or partnerships that have entered into working agreements with the major-league clubs to train and develop players. Under a Player Development Contract (Appendix B), the major-league club agrees to pay a certain portion of the minor-league club's operating expenses and player salaries. Although the standard contract is used by all clubs, many of the specifics are negotiated individually for each contract, forming a basis for competition among minor-league clubs seeking to become part of a particular major-league farm system.

Minor-league clubs are much smaller operations than the majors: a class A club may have an annual budget of about $120,000 and is often run by a single proprietor. Frequently, minor-league clubs are run as a sideline by local car dealers, store owners, or other businessmen. The price of admission to these games averages slightly more than $1, and average crowds range from 1,000 or so at lower levels up to 3,000 to 5,000 in some of the large AAA class cities.

For players and clubs, the minor-league system provides the training to convert high school and college athletes to players of major-league caliber. In this respect, professional baseball and hockey differ from football and basketball, where players are fully prepared by their college experience for the demands of playing in large-capacity stadia and the rigorous season schedule of professional sports. College baseball, in contrast, has attracted much less interest than college football or basketball. Although it is growing and improving, col-

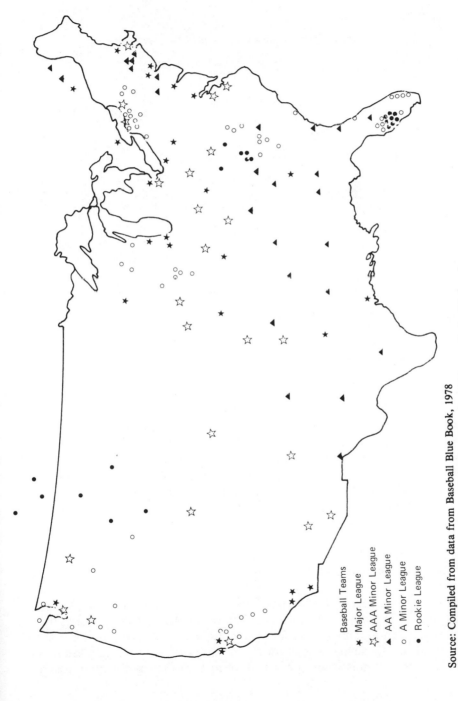

Source: Compiled from data from Baseball Blue Book, 1978

Note: There is also a Class AAA team in Honolulu, Hawaii and 20 teams in the Mexican League.

Figure 4-1. Location of Baseball Teams in the United States and Canada, 1978 Season

Baseball Teams
★ Major League
☆ AAA Minor League
◀ AA Minor League
○ A Minor League
● Rookie League

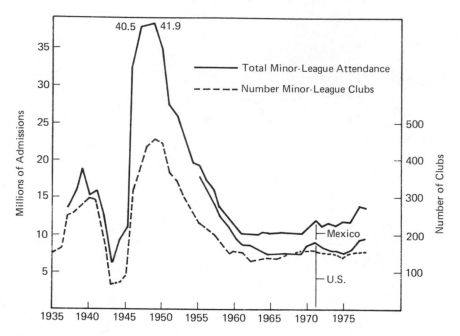

Source: National Association of Professional Baseball Leagues, *Highlights*, various years, and other records.

Notes: 1937-1945 are approximate; Mexican attendance broken out only after 1955.

Figure 4-2. Minor-League Baseball Attendance, 1937-1978

lege baseball has not provided the caliber of training needed for major-league play. Therefore, the minor leagues provide professional training that is not available elsewhere.

Each minor-league club, depending on its level, has twenty-one to thirty active players. Control of these players rests with the major-league parent: if a minor-league club shifts from one farm system to another, it is completely restocked with a new set of players in the new parent's farm system.

National Association of
Professional Baseball Leagues

The National Association of Professional Baseball Leagues (NAPBL) in St. Petersburg, Florida, performs a number of administrative functions for both the major and minor leagues. The president of the NAPBL occasionally is called "Commissioner of the Minor Leagues" and acts in a capacity similar to the commissioner of baseball for matters such as discipline arising in the minor leagues. The NAPBL also acts as a resource and an advisor in business matters for minor-league clubs.

Finally, the NAPBL through its large record-keeping operation maintains the official career records of all professional baseball players. The association is run by a small staff and is financed by fees charged to clubs for recording players' contracts.

As with the majors, much of the power in the minors resides with the leagues (for example, the Texas League, the International League, and so on). Control over franchises, umpiring, rule making, recordkeeping, and other functions remains in the hands of the league offices. Because they represent multiple levels of skill, the minor-league clubs operate more independently of one another than those in the majors.

Major League Baseball Promotion Corporation

The Major League Baseball Promotion Corporation (MLBPC) is a joint enterprise of the clubs which produces films, television shows, and publications about major league baseball, conducts national promotions for the sport, and operates a licensing program involving the clubs' names, logo types, insignia, and uniform designs. Cash proceeds from the MLBPC, after expenses are deducted, have been modest.

Playing Rules Committee

The Playing Rules Committee, which consists of three members from each league and three from the NAPBL, determines the playing rules which govern all games of major-league and NAPBL clubs. Any playing rule may be revised, repealed, or adopted by a two-thirds vote of this committee. With its assent, a league may adopt for itself an "experimental" rule which does not conform to the official rules.

The above are the major entities that together make up the *official* economic structure of professional baseball. In addition, there are a great many other enterprises that participate more or less directly in the total activity called baseball. These include American Legion baseball, the little leagues, and the Babe Ruth leagues, all of which are voluntary organizations that provide opportunities to play in organized baseball leagues. It might be added that professional baseball does, in fact, make annual donations to these activities. Also participating in the business of baseball are concessionaires at the ball park, public stadium authorities, publishers of baseball-related publications, players' agents, suppliers of equipment and materials, and the baseball-related portions of the press.

Flow of Funds through the Baseball Industry

An examination of the flow of dollars through the baseball industry demonstrates its structure and operation as well as the importance of relationships among the different participants.

Figure 4-3 shows the pattern of revenues and expenses.[1] The flows on the left-hand side of the diagram relate to activities directly involving the clubs themselves. Those on the right-hand side relate to joint enterprises and joint administration. As figure 4-3 shows, the major sources of revenues have been attendance at games ($144 million, counting spring training games, minor-league games, and end-of-season games), concessions, local TV and radio stations, and national network broadcasters. Total revenues of the industry amounted to $218 million. The principal expenses have been team operations, stadium operations, team replacement, player development, and general and administrative expenses. Joint sources of revenue, including national broadcasting royalties and all-star and end-of-season games, amounted to about $29 million, or 13 percent of the total. Joint expenses for league offices, umpires, the commissioner's office, the Major League Player Relations Committee, player benefits, and players' shares of World Series gate receipts amounted to more than $18 million, or about 9 percent of total expenses.

Not shown in the figure are any additional earnings that players might make (for example, through group licensing or personal appearances and endorsements). Also not shown are the capital investments of the clubs (for example, bonuses paid to free agents for signing contracts) or any amounts invested in facilities such as electronic scoreboards, stadium improvements, and the like. However, depreciation and amortization of these items are included in the appropriate expense categories, such as team or stadium operating expenses.

Figure 4-3 highlights the great dependence of baseball on the fans who go to the games. Table 4-2 regroups the sources of revenue. More than three-quarters of revenues came from fans at the ball park. If revenues from fans were divided by attendance, the average receipts to a club from the fans would amount to $5.16 per attendee. By way of comparison, the broadcasting revenues of about $44 million, when divided by the total local and national viewing audiences, would amount to a very small amount per fan.

On the expense side of the ledger, figure 4-3 illustrates the wide diversity of items for which baseball clubs spend their money. Table 4-3 regroups the expenses in a manner similar to the way table 4-2 did for revenues. Thus, about 34 percent of expenses went directly to players, and the remainder went to a variety of operating expenses and overhead. (Actually, the players' percentage is somewhat higher. An undetermined portion of contract payments and operating losses for minor-league clubs consists of

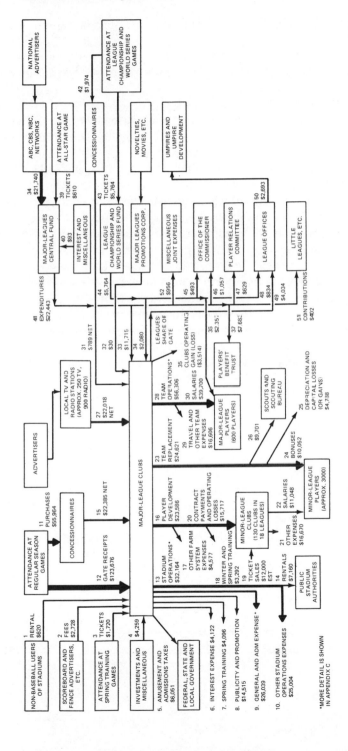

Amounts ($000) are averages of the 1975-1977 annual figures (twenty-four clubs).

Figure 4-3. Principal Revenues and Expenses in the Baseball Industry

salaries for players in clubs owned outright by a major-league parent.) Total expenses exceeded revenues by about $13 million per year, although this amount includes interest expense, investment income, and other non-operating items. From solely baseball operations, the major leagues lost an average of $3.5 million per year.

Systematic financial data were not available for minor-league clubs, but it is widely believed that these clubs on the whole also show a net loss.

Further, it has been estimated that the public stadium authorities that own most ball parks lose money—on the order of $23 million per year—although not all this loss would be attributable to baseball alone.[2]

One characteristic that figure 4-3 illustrates is the relative complexity of the flows of funds within baseball when one considers the relatively small size of the industry. While the aggregate revenues of baseball were only $218 million, there are literally hundreds of individual corporations in the United States with greater revenues. In financial terms, then, baseball is a small industry even when one considers such entertainments as nightclubs, phonograph records, sports-related magazines, and ski resorts. The fact that this flow was divided among twenty-four clubs, including more than one hundred minor-league clubs, concessionaires, stadium operators, and various intermediary units, makes baseball a more complicated enterprise than many people recognize.

Another distinguishing characteristic of baseball is the relative importance of joint sources of revenue and joint expenses. One can think of few other industries in which $1 of every $8 comes from a pooled source, partly because pooling would be inconsistent with policies insisting on the independence of competing firms.

Contracting with Players

Recruitment and Advancement

Professional baseball employs approximately 4,400 baseball players in the United States, Canada, and Mexico, of whom 650 are regular major-league

Table 4-2
Sources of Revenue

Item	Dollars (000)	Percentage
Fans via tickets	143,770	65.8
Fans via concessions	23,174	10.6
Broadcasters	43,758	20.0
Other	7,730	3.5
Total	218,432	100.0

The table is based on three-year averages (1975-1977).

Table 4-3
Expenses

Item	Dollars (000)	Percentage
Major-league players (salaries, benefits, and amortization of bonuses)	54,528	24.6
Minor-league players (salaries and bonuses)	21,100	9.5
Joint administration	8,405	3.8
Club administration	26,039	11.7
Stadium operations	32,164	14.5
Farm system and scouts	34,320	15.5
Team travel, operating expenses, and training	20,702	9.3
Marketing and other	24,688	11.1
Total	221,946	100.0

This table is based on the average of 1975 to 1977.

players, and 350 are minor-league players on major-league contracts. The remaining players are in about 130 U.S., Canadian, and Mexican minor-league clubs. A major-league player is active for about seven months each year, from the beginning of spring training in late February or early March until the end of the season in early October. Those who play in the league championship series and in the World Series have a more extended season. During the off-season, some players participate in the winter instructional league in Florida, or, with the permission of their clubs, play in Puerto Rico or other Latin American countries. During the off-season, some players may participate in speaking engagements or other publicity activities for their clubs. Otherwise, they are free to relax or seek other employment opportunities. Minor-league players play a shorter season—in some cases as short as three months—and are free to use the off-season as they wish.

Most professional baseball players are recruited upon graduation from high school, although a growing number are recruited from colleges and junior colleges. Baseball faces increasing external competition in the market for players. First, more and more high school athletes are going on to college. Many athletes who in earlier years might have tried out for the minors choose instead to take their chances on a college education. Among those who attend college, fewer are likely to end up pursuing a career in baseball. Second, the rapid growth over the past fifteen years of such other sports as football, hockey, basketball, and tennis has opened up other opportunities for persons with athletic ability. These newer sports may be more attractive than minor-league baseball because they can be combined with a college education, which increases an athlete's opportunities later in life. A number of people within baseball have reported that competition from other sports—particularly college football—has become an important factor in the scouting and recruiting of potential baseball players.

Once a player has entered professional baseball, his career may take a variety of forms. We have examined the careers of a random sample of 812 players who were active at some time between 1968 and 1977. The analyses presented in this section are drawn from that sample and from other sources.

About 48 percent of all players enter at the rookie level, and another 45 percent enter at the class A level. Some farm systems, such as that of the Los Angeles Dodgers, do not include any rookie clubs but instead have two or more class A clubs. (There are, in fact, certain gradations within the class A level that are remnants of the earlier structure which included class B, class C, and class D leagues. These gradations have been ignored in the current tabulations.) The remaining small percentage of players enter directly into class AA or AAA. Only four players, 0.5 percent of the sample, enter directly into the majors.

The normal progression for a player is to advance one level each year; thus he would spend a year in the rookie league, a year in class A, and so on, reaching the majors at the beginning of his fifth year. As a statistical average, this pattern is reasonably accurate: The average time needed to become a major-league player is, in fact, 4.6 seasons. However, few players conform to the average, and for an individual player the progression is seldom so simple. More often, he may be moved from one level to another several times within one season. Players are often traded from one club's farm system to another, and a player may therefore experience a dozen moves or more in progressing to the majors. Other players enter the field and are quickly successful. Figure 4-4 shows the actual pattern of movements for five selected players. Keeping in mind that each dot in the exhibit represents one month of playing time and that the seasons are typically seven months, it shows that player 1 during his second year played in class A, class AA, and class AAA, and during his third year he skipped back and forth twice between AA and AAA. He required two more years in class A, including being traded to another farm system, before he regained his class AAA status and then moved up to the majors. Player 5, by contrast, had a relatively simple pattern. He spent three years in class A, moved up to class AA for one year, and at the end of that year moved up to the big leagues, where he is still playing.

Figure 4-5 shows the annual flow of players through the ranks. In statistical terms, this figure is known as a Markov chain. The percentages adjacent to each box represent the fraction of players in that level who will have moved to the indicated level by March of the following year. Thus, within the rookie leagues, 28.1 percent of the players will begin the next season at the rookie level, 36.9 percent will move to class A, 4.9 percent will move to class AA, 1.5 percent will move to class AAA, and 1.7 percent will move directly to the major leagues. Some 26.9 percent will have been re-

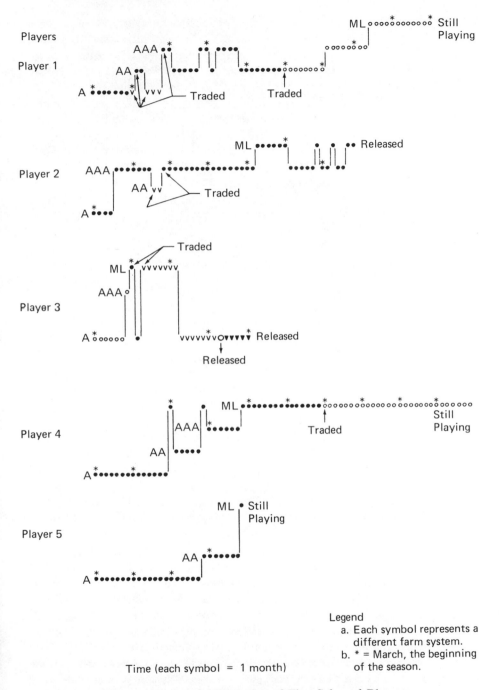

Figure 4-4. Career Histories of Five Selected Players

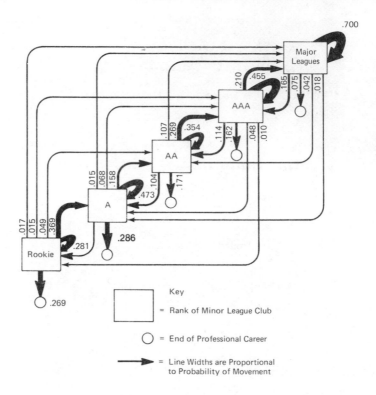

Source: Sample of 812 players careers.

Note: Flows of less than .010, that is, 1 percent, have been omitted.

Figure 4-5. Annual Flows of Players through the Ranks (Probabilities of Change in Rank from One Playing Season to the Next)

leased and not picked up by another farm system. Similarly, within class A, 47.3 percent will be again in class A, 15.8 percent will have moved up to class AA, and so on.

As might be expected, the highest dropout rates occur early in the system; both the rookie and class A levels reject more than one-quarter of their players each year. However, once a player reaches a major-league roster, he is by no means secure. A full 30 percent of major-league players will find themselves beginning the next season back in the minors or out of baseball altogether. In a sense, the rookie and class A leagues serve as an initial screen for players; very little promotion directly to the majors takes place from those levels. Once a player reaches class AA, his chances of promotion—or at least of retention—are much greater. From class AAA, a player is almost certain to be tried at least for a few games in the majors, and his chances of making the forty-man roster of a big league club within a few years are better than 50-50.

Table 4-4 and Figure 4-6 show the overall progression and survival of players in a somewhat different way. For an entering "class" of 812 players, they show how many would be at each level during succeeding years.[3] At the end of the first season, only 650 (about 80 percent) of the players would still be active in professional baseball. After two seasons the class would be down to about half its original size; after three seasons, one-third; after four seasons, one-quarter; after five seasons, one-fifth; and after seven seasons, one-tenth. As table 4-4 shows, practically none of the players would be left in the rookie league after two seasons, and very few would remain in class A after three seasons. At these levels, the pattern definitely is "up or out."

Note that table 4-4 should *not* be interpreted to mean that only 65 players from the entering group ever played in the majors. What it means is that *at any one time* the maximum number in the majors was 65. However, because of frequent movements up and down among levels, many more of the original group actually did see major-league service at one time or another—136, to be exact. In other words, *about one out of every six recruits entering professional baseball made it to a major-league roster* (the forty-man roster).

Only a fraction of players who reach the major-league forty-man roster are able to stay there for any length of time. About half play for one season or less (45 percent). Only about one out of four plays more than two

Table 4-4
Progression and Survival of Entering Players: Level as of March of Each Year

Year	Rookie	Class A	Class AA	Class AAA	Majors	Total
Entering year	393	367	28	20	4	812
1	180	327	63	53	27	650
2	28	185	99	71	34	417
3	4	43	69	110	52	278
4	2	18	32	85	65	202
5	1	12	28	54	63	158
6	—	5	19	48	54	126
7	—	6	16	27	40	89
10	—	3	5	10	26	44
15	—	—	1	5	11	17
20	—	—	—	—	2	2

Source: Tabulated from a sample of 812 players' careers (players who were active at some time between 1968 and 1977).

seasons, and long-term successes are indeed rare. *Only about one player out of fifty lasts more than six seasons.*

Contracting with Players—The Reserve System

Once a player chooses a career in baseball, his employment is governed by a complex set of agreements and rules known collectively as the *reserve system*. Major-league rules 3, 4, and 5 define the essential elements of this system, along with the major-league players' collective-bargaining agreement and numerous other rules that spell out specific details. In broad outline, the elements of these agreements governing a player's career path are as follows:

1. Twice a year, a *draft* is held at which clubs select "new" players, that is, athletes who have not previously played professional baseball. In these selections, major-league clubs (or their minor-league affiliates) take turns in reverse order of their league standings at the end of the previous season. The selecting club is granted a six-month exclusive op-

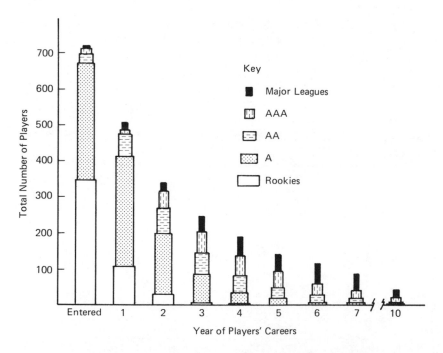

Figure 4-6. Survival and Progression of One "Class" of Baseball Players

portunity to negotiate a contract with the player. If these negotiations are unsuccessful, the player reenters the draft.

2.   Once a club has signed a player, it may, after each season, place him on its *reserve list* for the ensuing year, meaning that he may not play for or negotiate with any other club unless the reserving club agrees to assign or release his contract. A specific antitampering rule prohibits other clubs from approaching a reserved player to discuss employment without prior written approval from his current club.

3.   Limits are placed on the number of players a club may have on its reserve list. Subject to those limitations, clubs may trade or *assign* a player to other clubs. If they do so, the player is bound to serve the assignee (except in the case of certain veteran major-league players discussed below).

4.   To prevent hoarding of players, a special *rule 5 draft* allows clubs to draft certain players who are on the reserve lists of minor-league clubs. Operationally, this draft means that if a player has not advanced to a major league (forty-man) roster after four years in the minors (or sooner in certain circumstances), he becomes eligible to be drafted by other clubs. If a player is drafted under this rule, specified compensation—up to $25,000—must be paid to his former club.

5.   Veteran major-league players, with six years or more of major-league service, are exempted from some of the provisions of the reserve system. Most importantly, they can declare themselves *free agents*, able to negotiate with up to fourteen clubs for a new contract, and demand to be traded (or refuse a trade) if they meet certain length-of-service criteria.

A Uniform Player Contract is used for all minor-league players. Minimum salaries are $500 per month for rookie league players and progress in fixed steps up to $1,300 per month in class AAA. In addition, a player may be paid a bonus for signing a contract and receive certain conditional bonuses (for example, extra payment) if he is kept at least sixty days. In 1975, a total of $5,205,000 in bonuses was paid to 768 players, for an average bonus of about $6,800.[4]

The procedures for contracting with major-league players are decided through collective bargaining. The Major League Baseball Player Relations Committee negotiates for the clubs as the Major League Baseball Players' Association negotiates for the players. The contract, called the Basic Agreement, sets the terms of employment, benefits, minimum salaries, and other basic provisions of major-league players' employment. Most players earn considerably more than the minimum salary provided by the Basic Agreement. They negotiate these salaries individually with their clubs, or if a club and player cannot agree on a figure, the salary may be set by arbitration.

(The motion-picture industry has a somewhat similar type of collective-bargaining agreement. The basic contract sets minimum rates of pay, and performers individually negotiate higher rates of compensation.)

The 1976 Basic Agreement

Until 1976 the reserve system applied to major-league players for the entire length of their careers—that is, there were no provisions for a player to declare himself a free agent, he was bound to play for the same club (unless it decided to trade him). If a player felt he was underpaid, he could ask his club for more money or even take the matter to arbitration. But other than threatening to quit professional baseball, he had relatively little bargaining power. The 1976 Basic Agreement gives veteran players a much stronger bargaining position and, as a consequence, has made significant changes in the economics of baseball clubs.

Some type of entry-level draft is employed by all major-league sports. Its purpose is to maintain competitive balance by preventing wealthier clubs from buying up most of or all the promising talent, a problem that has existed from time to time in the past. (The development of baseball's amateur draft in 1965 often has been credited with breaking up the "Yankee dynasty" that dominated the American League for many years.) The earlier perpetual reserve system, moreover, was intended to reduce the tendency of better players to gravitate to the richest clubs; it created an incentive to invest in the development of young players, because clubs were guaranteed their use if they proved successful. A club, then, could either keep successful players or trade them to other clubs for cash or other players. The 1976 Basic Agreement greatly reduced this protection. As a consequence, many clubs turned to another device, the multiyear contract, to protect their investment in players. By 1978, about 80 percent of players with four or more years of major-league service had multiyear contracts.[5]

Figure 4-7 illustrates the clubs' obligations under player contracts that were in effect during the 1978 playing season. As the figure shows, the bulk of clubs' obligations under these contracts extended over the next four to five years. The great majority of future obligations were guaranteed; that is, the players would receive their payments regardless of injury, disability, or a decline in playing skill. This practice of guaranteeing future income and benefits has raised concern about the risk of clubs becoming burdened with "dead-wood" players who are past their playing prime (or simply not trying very hard) and still are receiving six-figure salaries. Although the possibility remains as a source of concern to many observers both inside and outside professional baseball, few if any instances have materialized.

Although multiyear contracts can slow down the gravitation of better players toward other, high-spending clubs, they obviously cannot prevent such moves altogether. Table 4-5 shows the trend in average player payroll per club in recent years. In 1974, the highest-spending five clubs spent approximately 1.6 times as much as the lowest-spending five clubs. By 1978 this ratio had increased to 2.5:1 and had raised considerable concern as to future prospects for competitive balance within the leagues. Unless there is some change in the present pattern, there is a danger that baseball will develop a two-tiered structure, with a few high-spending clubs dominating each league and the remaining ones more or less stuck below them in the standings.

Another result of the 1976 agreement has been the widening of the gap between the salaries of highly paid players and most other players. Figure 4-8 shows the distribution of players' compensation for the 1978 season. Under the terms of the Basic Agreement, the minimum salary for the 1978 season was $21,000, and as the figure shows, only about 5 percent of the players earned as little as the minimum. The largest group, one-fourth of the players, earned between $22,000 and $41,000. They accounted for roughly $5.3 million in compensation for the year. At the other end of the ladder, fourteen players (about 2 percent of the total) each earned $320,000 or more, and together they accounted for almost $6 million in compensation. In other words, these fourteen players earned more than 175 players at the lower end of the ladder.

The median salary during this season was about $70,000. Salaries had increased by 31 percent over the previous twelve months. This increase was almost entirely attributable to higher salaries rather than to having more players under contract. The number of players under multiyear contracts increased only from 321 to 324. Exactly 75 percent of these contracts were guaranteed.

Part of the range of variation in salaries was attributable to experience.

Table 4-5
Trend in Average Player Payroll per Club
($ million per year)

	1974	1975	1976	1977	1978
Average club	1.16	1.30	1.51	2.07	2.30
Highest five clubs	1.46	1.72	2.13	3.32	3.42
Lowest five clubs	0.89	0.78	1.10	1.22	1.36

Source: 1974-1976: clubs' financial survey, Schedule III. 1977: clubs' financial survey, Schedule IV. 1978: CRI tabulation of players' contracts for 1978 season.

Note: Figures include actual disbursements plus deferred compensation. The number of players per payroll may vary from year to year; for example, in 1978 payrolls included 651 players, compared to 685 in 1977, which explains the relatively small percentage change in the average payroll from 1977 to 1978 (11 percent).

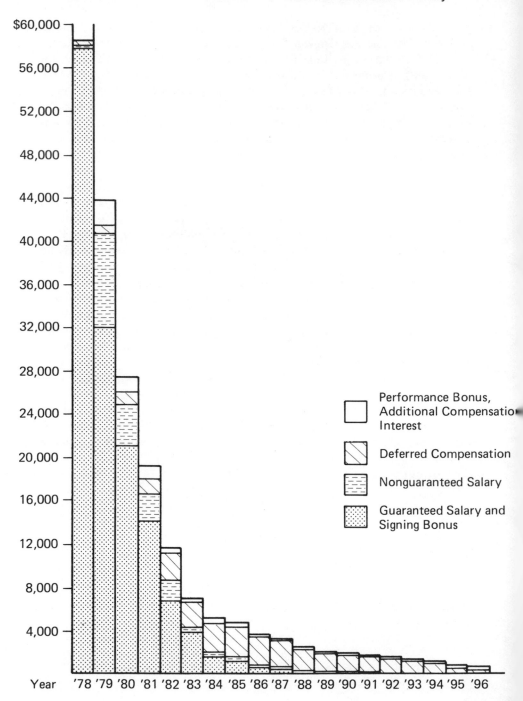

Figure 4-7. Major-League Cash Commitments under Player Contracts, 1978 ($000)

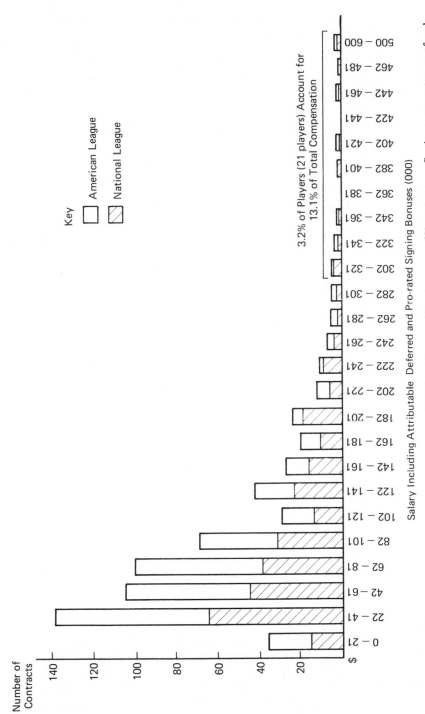

Source: Compiled from data supplied by American League and National League. The data cover 651 contracts, reflecting team rosters as of early June 1978.

Figure 4-8. Frequency Distribution of Major-League Salaries, 1978

There was a definite correlation between players' years of service and their compensation (see figure 4-9).

Market for Baseball Games

Another important market to consider in baseball is the market for games—what needs the industry serves and with what other firms and prod-

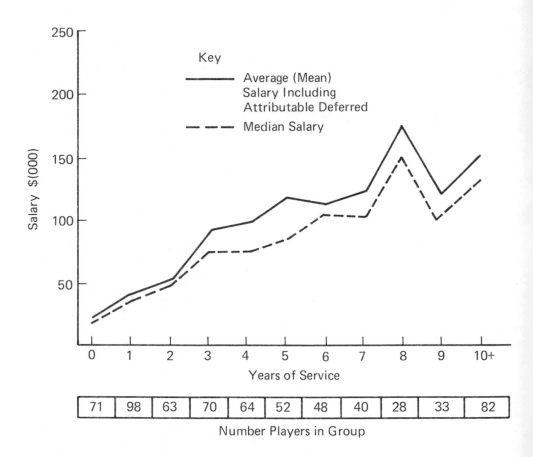

Source: Compiled from data supplied by American League and National League. Analysis is based on 651 contracts, reflecting team rosters as of early June 1978.

Figure 4-9. Average and Median Salary (Including Attributable Deferred), 1978

ucts it competes. Broadly speaking, baseball might be considered a form of entertainment, along with movies, nightclub acts, television shows, and other diversions or amusements. Some fans, of course, take their baseball more seriously. Baseball, more than any other sport, is known for its fans who can recite statistics, such as the batting averages of all the top players of the 1937 Yankees or the sequence of plays that won the third game of the 1962 World Series. Such a depth of knowledge ordinarily would not be associated with something that is considered only an entertainment or diversion. Rather, for these fans, baseball serves as a *hobby* of sorts. For other fans, baseball is a *symbol of community identification*. Bostonians could walk a little bit taller when the Red Sox won the American League Pennant in 1975, and unfortunately they could commiserate with one another when the team lost the World Series. New Yorkers in the mid-1960s, on the other hand, developed an unusual camaraderie through identifying with their underdog Mets. Baseball also serves a social role, providing a popular topic of discussion at social gatherings. Also of importance is the *role model* that players set for youngsters, and perhaps for the submerged hero in all of us.

As a leisure good, baseball, like many other traditional products, must compete in an increasingly differentiated and segmented market. Consumers today are faced with a wide array of activities that compete for their leisure time and discretionary dollars. As personal incomes rise, people tend to allocate a larger and larger share of their income to leisure goods. Whereas the local movie theater, the Saturday night dance, and the Sunday afternoon baseball game used to be staples of entertainment, today people have available a wide variety of both participant (tennis, skiing, bowling, backpacking, and so forth) and spectator sports (basketball, hockey, football, soccer, and so forth).

Television has played a major role in the development of spectator sports. Television offers viewers the option of watching sports in the comfort of their homes as an alternative to attending live performances. In addition to participant and spectator sports, numerous other leisure goods (travel, movies, theater, music, photography, and so on) compete for consumers' interest, time, and disposable income.

Spectator sports as a whole have benefited greatly as a result of increased leisure spending. Figure 4-10 shows this growth trend. Between 1960 and 1978 personal expenditures for spectator sports rose sixfold. Baseball has shared in this growth, but not at the same rate as some other sports (see figure 4-11). In 1950, major- and minor-league baseball achieved an attendance that was more than twenty times that of professional football. By 1978 the ratio was down to about 4:1, and basketball and hockey were drawing larger audiences than football.[6]

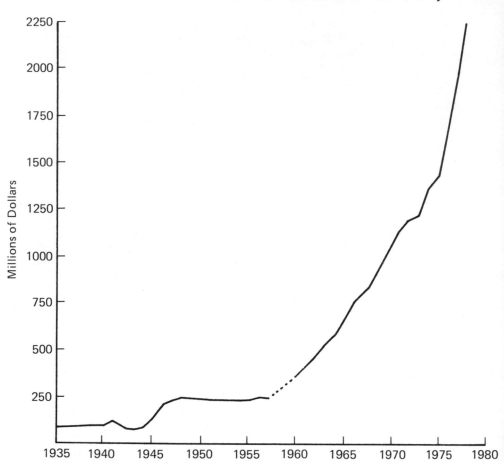

Source: *Statistical Abstract of the United States, 1978* (Washington: USGPO, 1978), and telephone conversations with U.S. Bureau of Economic Analysis personnel (February 23, 1979).

Note: Includes all sports for which admission is charged. The 1978 figure is estimated.

Figure 4-10. Estimated Personal-Consumption Expenditures for Spectator Sports, 1935-1978

It is not clear to what extent the growth in professional football, basketball, and hockey necessarily represents competition in the market for baseball's games. Because of the difference in playing seasons, it is possible that much of the growth in these other sports represents a new market and not a reduction in the growth of the baseball market. (Figure 4-12 compares the playing seasons of major team sports. Figure 4-13 shows the location of the major sports teams.) Although baseball overlaps with the basketball and hockey play-offs in the spring and with football preseason and early-season games in the late summer, there is a period of several months during which

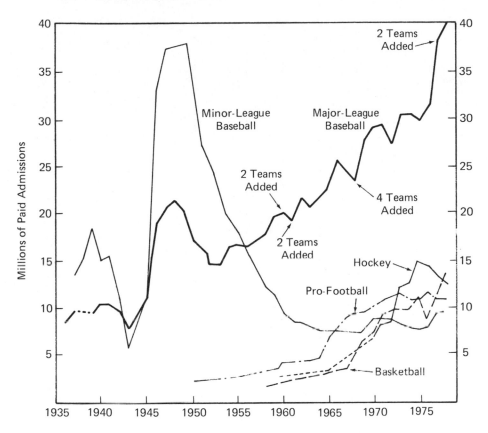

Sources: 1936-1977: *Statistical Abstracts of the United States* (Washington: USGPO, various years); 1978: league offices, National Association of Professional Baseball Leagues.

Note: Prior to 1955, minor-league figures include Mexican attendance, which at that time amounted to less than 1 million per year.

Figure 4-11. Attendance: Baseball, Basketball, Football, and Hockey, 1936-1978

baseball has little competition from other team sports. (Professional soccer, a relative newcomer, in the future may challenge baseball's dominance of sports attention during the summer. Its season overlaps the baseball season closely.)

It is possible, of course, that some fans who formerly attended only baseball games during the summer now spread their attendance over several sports throughout the year. It is also possible that other fans, whose community loyalties led them to follow their baseball team, have now been diverted to one of the newer football, basketball, or hockey teams. Figure 4-14 shows the growth in broadcasting revenues for major team sports. Figure 4-15 translates this growth into its financial impact on individual teams.

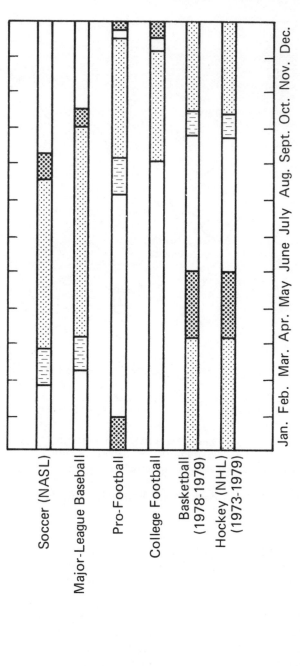

Sources: Telephone conversations with league offices and NCAA.

Note: The duration of some play-off periods is estimated. The duration of the exhibition season in soccer is estimated.

Figure 4-12. Seasons of Major Team Sports, 1979

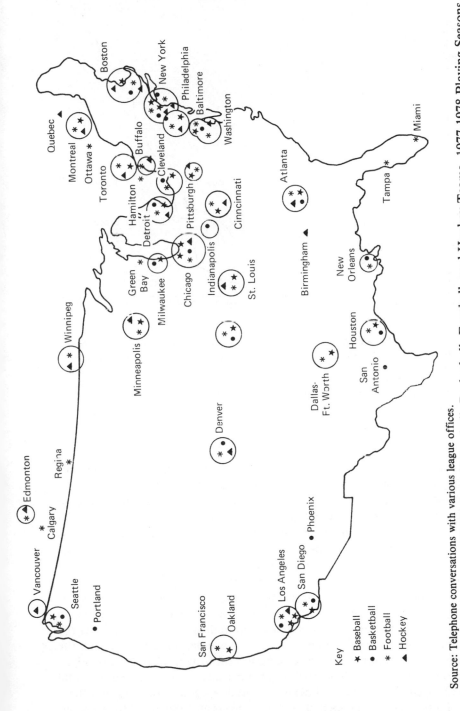

Source: Telephone conversations with various league offices.
Figure 4-13. Location of Professional Baseball, Basketball, Football, and Hockey Teams, 1977-1978 Playing Seasons

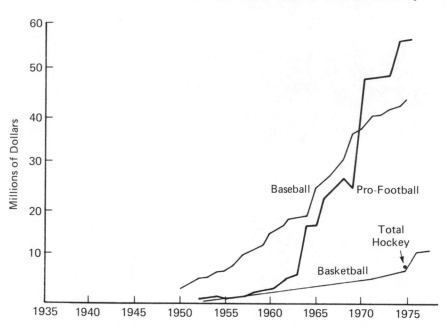

Sources: Roger G. Noll, ed., *Government and the Sports Business* (Washington: The Brookings Institution, 1974); U.S. Congress, House, Select Committee on Professional Sports, *Final
Report* (Washington: USGPO, 1976), p. 668.

Note: Football includes all play-offs and superbowl games, national and local. Baseball includes all regular and postseason games, national and local.

Figure 4-14. Total Broadcasting Revenues, Selected Professional Sports,
1950-1975

There are a few systematic studies regarding the competition among different professional sports for fans. One study of factors affecting attendance did find that the presence of "nonbaseball substitutes" tended to
reduce baseball attendance by about 300,000 for a metropolitan area
population of 2.5 million.[7] One source of time-series data on sports is the
annual Harris sports survey, published by the *Chicago Tribune*. These polls
show that the number of people who follow baseball and watch it on television has continued at about 55 to 60 percent of sporting fans.

Television-ratings data show a similar pattern, namely, that baseball is
holding its own or showing a modest growth in audience. The 1978 World
Series recorded one of the largest television audiences ever known. At the
same time, the audience ratings of college basketball have grown, and the
ratings of other major sports, after a period of growth, have held steady.

In summary, although baseball *might* have lost some fans (and potential
fans) to football, basketball, hockey, or other sports, it appears that these
other sports have mostly opened up new markets and expanded the total au-

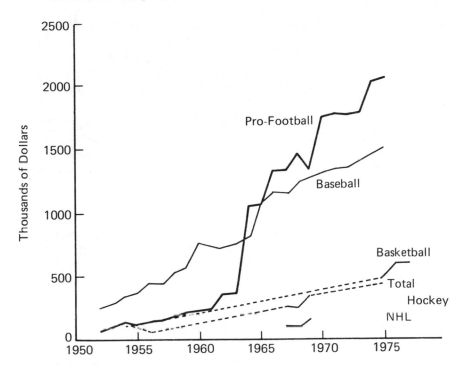

Source: U.S. Congress, House, Select Committee on Professional Sports, *Final Report* (Washington: USGPO, 1976), p. 668.
Note: Baseball and football include all regular and postseason games, national and local.
Figure 4-15. Broadcasting Revenue per Team, 1952-1977

dience for professional sports. The subject, we believe, remains one of high priority for further research. There are many interesting theories regarding consumers' tendencies to substitute one sport for another. These theories include a blue-collar effect, ethnicity effects, age-group theories, like-father-like-son effects, effects of climate, and so on. Unfortunately, most of these theories remain speculations until more empirical, systematic data become available.

Geographic Dimension

Baseball's market includes simultaneous local, regional, and national audiences. On the local level, one study found that the majority of spectators at baseball games come from within a 30-mile radius, with one-fourth to one-third of the fans coming from a greater distance.[8]

By and large, baseball clubs do not compete with one another for fans' attendance at games, because their markets are essentially local. The exceptions are the four two-team cities (Chicago, Los Angeles, New York, and San Francisco) where, in the San Francisco-Oakland market, for example, it appears that the two teams compete directly. Also, a few cities are close enough to have some fringe effects, such as Milwaukee and Chicago, or San Diego and Los Angeles (or Anaheim).

Some teams, such as the Boston Red Sox, the Philadelphia Phillies, and the Cincinnati Reds, appeal to a larger regional market and have corresponding regional broadcasting networks. For example, fans almost anywhere in New England can watch the Boston Red Sox games on television.

The competition for regional TV and radio audiences is complicated by both technology and institutional agreements. Each club has the exclusive right to broadcast its own games, both home and away, within its own home territory (defined as a 50-mile radius from its ball park). While the clubs are free to a degree to broadcast their own home games elsewhere in the country, in actual practice they have limited broadcasts and telecasts to that area which would normally be regarded as their regional trade territory and from which they could expect to attract fans to their park.

However, the growth of cable-television systems has added a new dimension of complexity and a new opportunity for competition. It is now possible, within the home territories of a number of major-league teams, to receive cable broadcasts of the games of other teams (without the need for consent of either the home club or the club being telecast). The competitor, in such a situation, is not the other team whose games are being shown. Rather, it is the cable-television operator who is picking up and redistributing the over-the-air signals of the out-of-town teams.[9]

At the national level, the major-league clubs jointly sell television rights for broadcasting of games on two dates each week on nationwide networks, as well as nationwide broadcasting of the all-star game, the league championship series games, and the World Series games. Clubs in all sports have taken steps to develop a national audience by pooling the sale of national TV rights.

Long-Term Trends in Market Coverage

Over the past twenty-five years, baseball has made a number of changes that have expanded its coverage of the market. Most significant of these is the expansion of the number of cities being served. In 1950, there were ten metropolitan areas with baseball teams, of which four (Boston, Chicago, Philadelphia, and St. Louis) had two teams and one (New York) had three teams. By 1978 there were twenty-two metropolitan areas being served, again with four having two teams (Chicago, Los Angeles, New York, and San Francisco-Oakland). Another change has been the expansion of night games, with the result that by 1976 more than half of all games were played at night. Other changes were the extension of the season from 154 to 162 games, the addition of the league championship play-off games at the end of the season, new and larger parks for most clubs, and increased broadcasting schedules, so that by now virtually all games are carried by radio and more than half by telecast.

However, in spite of these expansions, average annual attendance per team over the past twenty-five years has shown slow growth, as shown in table 4-6.

Market Potential

One of the questions that has arisen concerning the market for baseball games is whether there are large cities which could support more baseball activity than they now do or cities without teams which could, in fact, support them. This has played a prominent role in the debate over baseball's antitrust immunity. If indeed there is a great amount of market potential that is currently unexploited because of the leagues' control over franchise allocation, then this control might be considered a use of monopoly power for the purpose of protecting the leagues' own financial interest. If cities that have been unable to obtain teams in the past are demonstrably capable of supporting a team, then the present rules have unduly restricted entry.

However, if there appears to be little room for increased baseball activity, then completely unregulated addition of new teams would greatly disrupt the sport, since further division of the market would send many existing teams and new teams entering marginal market areas into financial

Table 4-6
Average Regular-Season Attendance per Club, 1950-1978

Year	Number of Clubs	Total Attendance	Average Attendance per Club-All Clubs
1950	16	17,463,000	1.091
1960	16	19,911,000	1.244
1970	24	28,747,000	1.198
1975	24	29,790,000	1.241
1976	24	31,318,000	1.305
1977	26	38,710,000	1.489
1978	26	40,637,000	1.563

Sources: Attendance figures are from *The Sporting News Official Baseball Guides* and th Baseball Commissioner's Office, final official attendance records.

turmoil. All clubs, of course, would bear some of the costs of unprofitable teams. Some marginally profitable teams would probably fold, and the entry of too many marginal teams would create an intolerable drain on the rest of the clubs, threatening their stability and continuity. Therefore, the market potential for baseball is important to any analysis of baseball's economic performance.

In order to reach some understanding of long-term trends in the market for baseball, we undertook a brief series of analyses (specifically, a set of regression equations) to determine the variables affecting attendance over a twenty-five-year period, and we compared our conclusions with those of two other studies on this subject, by Noll and Demmert.[10]

The factors selected for analysis were population of the city,[11] team performance, demographic factors of the city (for example, income level, proportion of black and elderly people), ticket prices, presence of other major sports teams, and age of the stadium.

Our findings were similar to those of earlier studies. Population was the single most important factor affecting attendance,[12] but while we found that there is no *fixed* proportion between population and attendance, attendance *per capita* is much higher in small cities than in larger ones.[13] Attendance in small cities sometimes was as much as or more than that of teams in cities six to eight times their size. (Figure 4-16 shows per capita attendance for major-league cities in 1975.) For this reason, it is very difficult to determine the exact population required to support a team. There is little consistency in per capita attendance rates among the smallest baseball cities, which indicates that exogenous factors (for example, the presence of other entertainments and other cultural interests) are responsible for these variations in attendance rates.

On the basis of our financial analysis (see chapter 5), we have found that it took, during 1975, roughly $5 million in annual revenues for a team to break even (or an attendance of about 1 million per year). The regression analysis suggests that a population of approximately 1.25 million is needed to achieve this attendance (a per capita attendance of about 0.8 for cities in this size range), other things being equal. The problem is that "other things" are not equal among baseball cities—or even in one city over time. Cincinnati is a good example of a club whose attendance far exceeded the average (in figure 4-16 it represents the highest attendance, at about 1.85 attendees per capita). Atlanta, Pittsburgh, and Houston fell considerably below average. The trend of baseball economics, as discussed in chapter 5, has been toward even higher revenues required for breakeven.

There are a number of unoccupied market areas that might have sufficient population to support a baseball team. These include such cities as Buffalo, Miami-Fort Lauderdale, Denver, Washington, Indianapolis, Newark, New Orleans, and Tampa-St. Petersburg. However, several of the

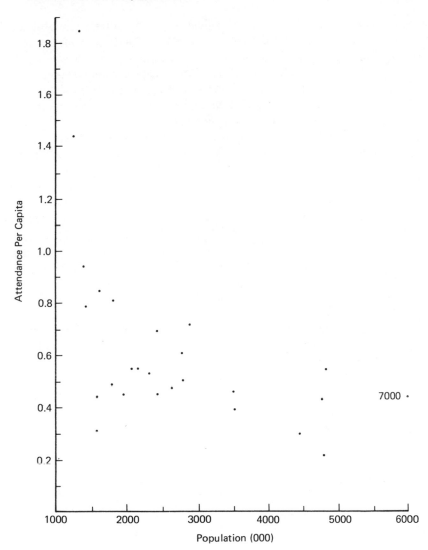

Note: In cities with two teams, the population is divided in half.

Figure 4-16. Attendance per Capita versus City Size, 1977

current major-league cities have populations that, in theory, might not be sufficient to support a club, including Atlanta, Kansas City, Milwaukee, San Diego, and, for two teams, San Francisco-Oakland. Judging the specific factors that would enable each area to support a team would require a much more detailed study.

The San Francisco-Oakland case illustrates the pattern in two-team areas. Since 1968, the San Francisco Giants and the Oakland Athletics have shared the Bay Area market, with unfortunate results for both teams. Table 4-7 shows attendance figures from 1958-1968, when only the Giants played in the area. Table 4-8 and figure 4-17 show attendance trends for the Giants and the Athletics when both teams played there. Since 1968, when the Athletics came to the area, the Giants have drawn 1 million fans only twice (in 1971 and 1978). Before 1968, the Giants' attendance consistently passed the 1 million mark; in the ten preceding years it averaged 1,499,000. On the other hand, the highest attendance figure ever reached by the Athletics was 1,078,000 in 1975. This was the year after the three consecutive years in which Oakland won the World Series (1972, 1973, and 1974). (During these years, as well as in 1975, the Giants' attendance fell off sharply, barely clearing 500,000 in 1974 and 1975.)

The combined attendance of the two teams seldom exceeded 1.8 million, and, in fact, it declined, on the average, from 1969 to 1977. However, the Giants enjoyed a strong resurgence in 1978, and on the basis of this showing some Bay Area boosters insisted that the area could indeed support two clubs. Nevertheless, the eleven-year record seemed unpromising.

Team performance emerged as the second most important factor influencing attendance. By using the number of games behind the pennant winner at the end of the preceding season, it was found that the coefficients on games out of first place ranged between 19.5 and 27.6, which means that a team that was one game closer to the winner at the end of the season would have added between 19,500 and 27,600 spectators. These results indicate that the extent to

Table 4-7
Giants' Attendance, 1958-1967

Year	San Francisco
1958	1,272,625
1959	1,422,130
1960	1,795,356
1961	1,391,221
1962	1,592,594
1963	1,571,316
1964	1,504,000
1965	1,546,000
1966	1,657,000
1967	1,242,000
Total	14,994,242
Average	1,499,000

Source: Compiled from data from *The Baseball Encyclopedia* (New York: The Macmillan Co.), 1976.

Table 4-8
Attendance for Oakland Athletics and San Francisco Giants, 1968-1978

Year	Athletics	Giants	Total Bay Area (Both Clubs)
1968	837,000	837,000	1,674,000
1969	778,000	874,000	1,652,000
1970	778,000	741,000	1,519,000
1971	915,000	1,106,000	2,021,000
1972	921,000[a]	648,000	1,569,000
1973	1,001,000[a]	834,000	1,835,000
1974	846,000[a]	520,000	1,366,000
1975	1,078,000	523,000	1,601,000
1976	781,000	627,000	1,408,000
1977	496,000	700,000	1,196,000
1978	527,000	1,740,000	2,267,000

Source: Compiled from data from *The Sporting News Official Baseball Guide*; baseball commissioner's office.

[a]Pennant year.

which a team can remain a pennant contender will have a significant effect on attendance figures. A poorly performing team, even in a very good market, could expect relatively low attendance.

We also evaluated the effects of several demographic characteristics on attendance. Although it has often been observed that baseball audiences tend to be from lower-income groups, our findings did not bear this out.[14]

Others have observed, as mentioned earlier, that blacks tend to be underrepresented in baseball attendance. To check this more systematically, we included the racial composition of a city as an independent variable. The variable turned out to have significance only in 1950, when it had a negative coefficient; that is, as the proportion of black population increased overall, attendance at games decreased. No effect was observed in more recent years.

The proportion of elderly is highly correlated with both income and race, and therefore it was not possible to assess the individual weight of the effect of the elderly population on attendance. However, age did show up as a strong positive variable affecting attendance for the "1960 teams in 1970" (that is, in older baseball cities).

The ticket-price variable was a weighted average of prices asked. However, the data give no indication of the proportion of seats sold, by price, and one way in which clubs might increase revenue without changing posted prices is to alter their mix of low-price versus high-price seats. Using this somewhat limited data, our regressions did not show a significant relation between attendance and ticket prices, and thus the matter remains inconclusive. (This observation must be qualified by the fact that ticket prices and income, which also appears in the equation, were strongly correlated.)

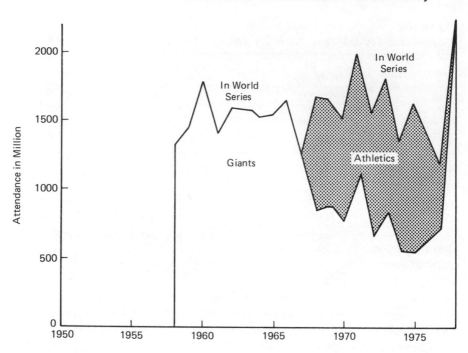

Figure 4-17. San Francisco-Oakland Baseball Attendance, 1958-1978

Finally, we found that stadium age was significant (and predictably positive) only in 1970. Even if our results had indicated more strongly that the newness of stadia positively affects attendance, it would be difficult to judge the extent to which promotional activities that commonly accompany a new or renovated stadium opening cause the increase. Nevertheless, the building of a new stadium appears, in practical experience, to increase attendance.

Summary

Of the variables thought to affect baseball attendance, it is clear that the size of the market, as measured by population, is critical. If a team is to sell an average of 1 million seats per year, a city of at least 1.25 million is necessary to support a team. Few cities of this size currently lack a team. Accordingly, expansion prospects are limited. Therefore, questions necessarily are raised regarding the prospects for survival of existing teams in smaller cities. Also, since the breakeven revenues and attendance have risen since 1975 (the base year selected for this particular computation), an even larger population would appear to be necessary.

The importance of closely matched teams is also vital. The extent to which a team can remain a pennant contender will have a significant effect of attendance figures.

The demographic composition of a city seems to have relatively little effect on attendance. Baseball appears to appeal to a wide cross section of the population, with relatively modest differences in interest noticeable among different types of fans. Furthermore, it appears that the patterns of even these differences are becoming less distinct than they once were.

Other variables do affect baseball attendance; the fact that these have altered over the twenty-five-year period studied suggests that the audience itself has changed. Tastes have changed, recreation options have changed, and the structure of city populations has changed (by age, race, and ethnicity). A slow, steady growth in attendance per team has been maintained even as the number of baseball cities has risen from ten in 1950 to twenty in 1970-1975. The extent and types of approaches needed in the future to ensure attendance growth will have to reflect the changes that have been occurring during the postwar period.

Notes

1. Sources and additional detail for some items in this exhibit are given in Appendix C. Amounts shown are annual averages for the 1975-1977 period.

2. Roger N. Noll, ed., *Government and the Sports Business* (Washington: The Brookings Institution, 1974), p. 345.

3. These 812 players entered professional baseball over a period of eight years. This fact causes a slight downward bias in the survival rates shown in table 4-4 and figure 4-6, inasmuch as the more recent entrants had not yet had sufficient time to reach higher levels.

4. Letter from Robert R. Bragan, president of the National Association of Professional Baseball Leagues, to Congressman Frank Horton; reprinted in U.S. Congress, House, Select Committee on Professional Sports, *Final Report* (Washington: USGPO, 1976), pt. 1, p. 344.

5. Murray Chass, "Few Cases Seen in Which Initiative Blunted by Long-Term Contract," *The New York Times*, March 5, 1978.

6. Professional baseball enjoyed a tremendous boom in the years just after World War II, which somewhat distorts the comparisons made above. Nevertheless, the basic conclusions are valid, as is evident from the graphs of attendance and revenue.

From 1945 to 1950, major-league attendance doubled beyond its prewar average. The gain in the minor leagues was even greater. In 1949, the peak year, minor-league attendance exceeded 40 million, and there were approximately 450 minor-league teams in fifty-nine leagues. As the graphs show, major-league attendance dropped sharply in the early 1950s and began a more steady progression, while minor-league attendance fell steadily.

Some observers attribute the minor-league decline to the effects of nationwide telecasts of major-league baseball games, which began in 1950. However, it probably is misleading to draw such comparisons. The late 1940s were a period of unprecedented growth in many aspects of U.S. life, including birthrates, suburban home development, automobile ownership, and even light-aircraft production. Growth in all these sectors subsided to more reasonable levels in the ensuing years. This does not mean that they were "performing poorly," but were merely a reflection of the abnormal situation that existed in many parts of the U.S. national economy in the immediate postwar years.

7. Henry G. Demmert, *The Economics of Professional Team Sports* (Lexington, Mass.: Lexington Books, D.C. Heath and Co., 1973), p. 68.

8. Pittsburgh Chamber of Commerce, "The Impact of Baseball on the Pittsburgh Economy," 1977, p. 8; also Baltimore Orioles, *Baltimore Baseball Club Survey, 1954*, p. 7.

9. Only about one out of six U.S. households is presently connected to a cable-television system, and only a few cities as yet have signficiant importation of out-of-town games. Boston is one example. In 1977 about 180 games of the New York Yankees and the New York Mets were available to cable viewers in Boston, along with 100 over-the-air games of the Boston Red Sox.

Cable-television systems are expected to grow significantly. Some forecasters expect they will reach about 30 percent of U.S. households in the mid-1980s. To attract these new households, cable operators are likely to seek additional sports programs, such as out-of-town games.

10. Noll, *Government and the Sports Business*, pp. 115-154; Demmert, *Economics of Professional Team Sports*.

11. The term *city* is used interchangeably with *metropolitan area*. Data presented for baseball cities are for the relevant standard metropolitan statistical areas (SMSAs). Montreal has been omitted from some parts of the analysis because Canadian census data were unavailable at the time of the study.

12. The only period for which city size was not a signficant factor was 1950, when baseball was enjoying a wave of national popularity. The insignificance of the variable in this period is therefore not surprising.

13. Over time, however, the relationship has shifted. In 1950 there were wide variations in per capita attendance among cities of comparable population (or population per team). By 1975, most cities were clustered into a narrower range of per capita attendance, even though their sizes were more varied than before. This pattern suggests that attendance has become a somewhat more stable percentage of the population.

14. Such a phenomenon could stem from a number of causes, such as the comparatively low ticket prices. We found that income was positively related to attendance in 1950 and 1960 and negatively related in 1975. This suggests that there has been a shift in the income effect over time, perhaps because baseball had fewer competitors in the earlier period. In all years the observed income effect was small in comparison with the effects of city size and team performance.

5

Financial Performance of Baseball Clubs 1974-1978

Introduction

How well does a baseball club perform as a business? Is it a good investment? What are the opportunities and the risks of operating a club? These kinds of questions have been asked for many years by baseball fans, sports writers, and others interested in the game. Interest in clubs' finances has probably been heightened by the fact that practically all clubs are privately held, being owned either by a single individual, partnerships, or by closed corporations with just a few stockholders. The absence of publicly available financial information has led to speculation about fat profits, high-expense-account living, and mysterious tax gimmicks that allow owners to pursue their hobbies at the taxpayers' expense. The mystery and secrecy surrounding the game and its personalities contribute in part to its glamour and excitement. Given the relatively small size of clubs as business enterprises, it seems doubtful that their finances would attract as much interest if they were published in annual reports issued to investors.

From time to time, the public has gained glimpses into the finances of clubs. For example, industry testimony during the Celler committee hearings in the early 1950s and again before the Sisk Committee in 1976 presented a variety of financial data both for the industry as a whole and for individual clubs. *Broadcasting Magazine* has annually published a rundown on the revenues that clubs receive from local radio and television broadcasting (although these data need careful interpretation). One club, the Chicago Cubs, issues its financial statements annually, and for many years the Baltimore Orioles did also. Occasionally, financial data for particular clubs may come to light in press stories, as happened during the controversy surrounding the sale of the Boston Red Sox in 1978.

The Sisk Committee's final report made it clear that the committee considered the mystery surrounding clubs' finances to be a major factor operating against continuation of the antitrust immunity:

> This Committee has had no opportunity to evaluate baseball's argument that continued exemption from the antitrust laws may be economically justified. . . . There has been a history of reluctance on the part of the industry to voluntarily share its financial information. . . . For this reason, among others, we will recommend that a successor to this Committee be directed to conduct an in-depth industry economic analysis.[1]

The information presented in this chapter is based on a survey of the revenues and expenses for all clubs for 1974 to 1978. We questioned clubs on revenues from all sources, expenses of all types, and a number of non-financial matters, such as the number of games that were telecast. A copy of the survey questionnaire, showing all questions asked, is included in Appendix A.

Starting in the early 1970s, a number of the clubs' controllers began developing a uniform chart of accounts to aid in comparisons of club data. At the time of this survey, many of the clubs had converted to using this system, and others expected to convert in the near future. The survey questionnaire was developed from that uniform chart of accounts.

All data provided by the clubs were mailed directly to an independent accounting firm, Ernst and Whinney, for tabulation. The survey itself, however, was not audited. Ernst and Whinney made a variety of consistency checks on the data on the basis of their experience as auditors for a number of clubs. Some minor adjustments were made for purposes of comparability (for example, matters relating to the timing of fiscal years).

Summary of Findings

Profitability

The profit picture of baseball provides a mosaic of contrasts. Several clubs had losses of $2 million per year or more during the period surveyed. (Note that there were only twenty-four clubs prior to 1977.) The largest group of clubs exhibited losses that ranged from zero to $1 million per year. Table 5-1 shows the distribuiton of net baseball income before taxes for 1974 to 1977. The top half of this table shows the number of clubs falling into different income categories for each year, and the bottom half shows the average for all clubs, as well as the median, and totals for each league and for both leagues combined.

Major-league baseball as a whole has shown losses ranging up to $7 million per year in recent years. There appear to be two countervailing trends: as the National League declined from a $4 million profit to a $5 million loss, the American League improved its position from a loss of $11 million to a profit of $3.7 million. This pattern relates closely to the attendance trends in the two leagues, as discussed below.

In 1978, a season of record attendance, the American League showed a profit of $222,000 and the National League lost $256,000, for a combined total loss of $34,000. Twelve clubs earned a profit, and fourteen showed losses—a pattern very similar to that of 1977.

Table 5-1
**Distribution of Net Income before Taxes[a] (from Baseball Operations Only),
1974-1977**

| | | Number of Clubs | | |
		1974	1975	1976	1977
Profit:	$2 million plus	2	1	1	2
	$1 million to $2 million	0	2	3	5
	$0 to $1 million	5	7	3	4
Loss:	$0 to $1 million	13	8	10	6
	$1 million to $2 million	3	4	5	6
	$2 million plus	1	2	2	3
		24	24	24	26
Average profit (loss)		(284)[b]	(184)	(194)	(108)
Median		(347)	(77)	(311)	(230)
American League clubs combined		(11,168)	(5,324)	(1,799)	3,662
National League clubs combined		4,221	912	2,848	(6,480)
24-Club Total[c]		(6,947)	(4,412)	(4,647)	(2,818)

Source: Tabulation from Schedule X of clubs' financial survey.

[a]Does not include interest expense or income from nonbaseball sources such as invetments; also does not include the small net gain or loss of the Major League Central Fund, a nonprofit organization.

[b]Dollar amounts are in thousands.

[c]In 1977 there were twenty-six clubs.

Figure 5-1 presents the income information in bar-chart form and also compares the income for these seasons with data presented before Congress some years ago concerning the 1965 season.[2] An interesting characteristic observable in this figure is that the pattern of profits and losses has changed very little, either in shape or in the dollar amounts, from the pattern exhibited in 1965.

Attendance is the largest factor explaining variations among clubs' net earnings. This is particularly true when net earnings are adjusted to take out the effects of player depreciation (see figure 5-2). Under current tax laws, the amount of player depreciation can vary significantly depending on how recently the club changed ownership. Thus, the data in figure 5-2 reflect the approximate *cash-flow* profitability of clubs. (Depreciation of players' contracts is by far the largest component of clubs' depreciation. Depreciation for office equipment and similar items has not been added back into the points plotted in figure 5-2.) The operating breakeven of clubs appears to have advanced from about 1.0 million in attendance in 1974-1976 to about 1.2 million in 1977.

Over half of the clubs in each season showed a loss: thirteen in 1975, fourteen in 1978, and fifteen in the other years. Furthermore, there was a relatively wide variation in the net income among clubs. Individual clubs might shift from showing a profit in one year to reporting a loss in the

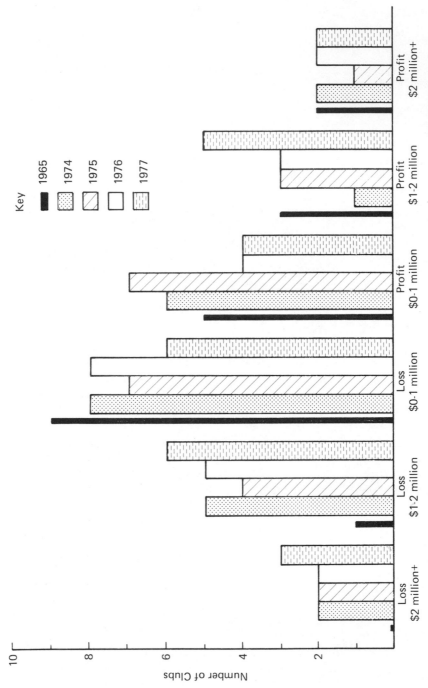

Source: 1974-1977: Tabulation from Schedule X of clubs' financial survey; 1965: *Hearings before the House Judiciary Committee*, 1965.

Figure 5-1. Distribution of Net Income before Taxes (from All Operations), 1974-1977

Earnings Plus Interest and
Player Depreciation ($000)

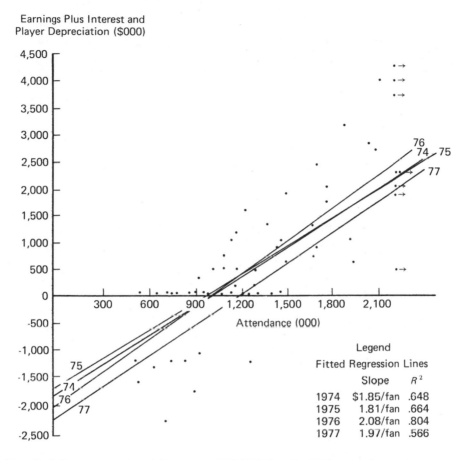

Figure 5-2. Earnings plus Interest and Player Depreciation versus Attendance, 1974-1977

Note: Each dot represents one club one year, 1975-1977. Dots for 1974 are not shown. Arrows indicate that the dot actually occurs at a higher attendance but has been moved to 2.2 million to protect confidentiality.

next, even though the relative number of clubs in each category had not changed substantially. Indeed, there were a couple of dramatic changes in the fortunes of individual clubs during the seasons surveyed.

The scattergram in figure 5-2, showing net cash flows other than depreciation of physical assets, further illustrates this wide variation in clubs' earnings. The band within which all clubs may be found had a width of about $2 million. That is, for a given attendance, some clubs earned $2 million more than some others. If we consider the fact that most clubs' revenues were only in the range of $5 million to $9 million, this is a *wide* band, on the order of 25 percent of revenues. There appears to be no simple explanation for these variations. Ranges of proportionate width occurred in clubs' expenses for salaries, stadium operations, and player development, and similarly for revenues from television, concessions, and the like.

The fitted regression lines on this figure indicate that clubs earned, on the average, an additional $1.81 to $2.08 in cash flow for each additional fan at the ball park.

How attractive are baseball clubs as investments? What is their rate of return? We do know from press reports that changes of ownership during the 1970s carried pricetags ranging between about $8 million (San Francisco Giants) and about $18 million (Boston Red Sox). Let us say, moreover, using a rough approximation, that the average price of these clubs was about $12.5 million. Further, let us assume that the *highest*-earning clubs (in the $2 million-plus category) averaged about $2.5 million per year. This would work out to a rate of return on market value of about 20 percent before taxes, a relatively mediocre rate of return by most industry standards. By way of comparison, major corporations such as General Motors and General Electric have often earned rates of return on equity close to that level *after* taxes. Keep in mind, however, that we used for this example the earnings of the *top* baseball clubs. All others fell below that level of return; indeed, most of them showed a net loss.

Depreciation and Tax-Shelter Considerations

There is, of course, another way in which owners might convert a mediocre pretax rate of return into an attractive investment, and that is through the mechanism of tax shelters. The only significant tax shelter available in professional sports has been the depreciation of players' contracts. When an owner purchased a sports franchise, a portion of the purchase price could be designated as the remaining value of players' contracts, and this amount depreciated over a period of perhaps five or six years. (The portion of purchase price that could be so designated was, of course, an important variable to the Internal Revenue Service, which has exerted increasing pressure over the years to reduce that fraction. The owners of the Atlanta Falcons football team once attempted to allocate as much as 90 percent of their purchase price to player contracts, but only 39 percent was allowed by the courts.)

For this type of shelter to be exploited, a new club must be sold every six or seven years so that a new owner can begin anew the depreciation of the players' contracts. Such a phenomenon appears to have developed in some other sports, with an increasing rate of turnover of club ownership. In baseball, however, clubs have not changed hands rapidly (see tables 5-2 and 5-3). The median length of ownership in January 1979 was 8 years in the American League and 14.5 years in the National. Of the sixteen clubs that comprised the majors for many decades, six remained under the same ownership in 1979 as they had had in the early 1950s. Among the ten teams created since 1960, six remained under original ownership. Further, many of the transfers of ownership in baseball were prompted by unusual events, such as the death of an owner (Boston) or major financial duress (San Diego or Seattle). Since this study was completed, an additional six clubs have changed ownership: the Houston Astros, the New York Mets, the Baltimore Orioles, the Chicago White Sox, the Oakland Athletics, and the Seattle Mariners. Although these franchise sales increase baseball's turnover ratio, there is little if any prospect that they were motivated by the types of tax shelter being discussed here. The Tax Reform Act of 1976 and subsequent tax changes have effectively eliminated the possibilities for such shelter.

As a test of the impact of depreciation on clubs' reported earnings, we computed a pretax cash flow and compared this with depreciation amounts. Pretax cash flow is the total amount of funds left over after operations, before any interest or taxes are paid and before any adjustments are made for capital expenditures or capital-consumption allowances. If the federal tax regulations did not allow depreciation, then pretax cash flow would be the amount on which a club was taxed. For any business, some allowances (in the form of depreciation) must be made for consumption of capital,

Table 5-2

Length and Form of Ownership of Major-League Baseball Clubs, January 1, 1979, National League

Club	Form of Ownership	Date Present Ownership Took Control	Length of Ownership (Years)
Chicago Cubs	Ordinary corporation	1932	47
Philadelphia Phillies	Ordinary corporation	1943	36
Los Angeles Dodgers	Ordinary corporation	1950	29
Pittsburgh Pirates	Ordinary corporation	1950	29
St. Louis Cardinals	Ordinary corporation	1953	26
New York Mets[a]	Subchapter S. corporation	1962	17
Cincinnati Reds	Ordinary corporation	1967	12
Montreal Expos[b]	Canadian partnership	1969	10
San Diego Padres[b]	Subchapter S. corporation	1974	5
Atlanta Braves	Ordinary corporation	1975	4
San Francisco Giants	Partnership	1977	2
Houston Astros[a]	Ordinary corporation	1978[c]	1

[a]Expansion team created in 1962.

[b]Expansion team created in 1969.

[c]There was no change in tax status resulting from this ownership change.

Table 5-3
Length and Form of Ownership of Major-League Baseball Clubs, January 1, 1979, American League

Club	Form of Ownership	Date Present Ownership Took Control	Length of Ownership (Years)
Minnesota Twins	Ordinary corporation	1920	59
Oakland Athletics	Ordinary corporation	1961	18
Detroit Tigers	Subchapter S. corporation	1961	18
California Angels[a]	Ordinary corporation	1961	18
Baltimore Orioles	Ordinary corporation	1965	14
Kansas City Royals[b]	Subchapter S. corporation	1969	10
Milwaukee Brewers[b]	Limited partnership	1970	9
Cleveland Indians	Limited partnership	1972	7
New York Yankees	Limited partnership	1973	6
Texas Rangers[a]	Limited partnership	1974	5
Chicago White Sox	Ordinary corporation	1975	4
Toronto Blue Jays[c]	Limited partnership	1977	2
Seattle Mariners[c]	Partnership	1977	2
Boston Red Sox	Limited partnership	1978	1

[a]Expansion team created in 1961.
[b]Expansion team created in 1969.
[c]Expansion team created in 1977.

since this is a real cost of doing business. Such allowances are a reasonable and proper way of allowing business to recover its capital for reinvestment. However, during the Sisk hearings, a number of witnesses implied that some baseball owners were using the depreciation from their clubs to shelter income from other sources. By comparing pretax-cash-flow amounts with actual depreciation charges, we attempted to develop a measure of the extent to which clubs might be able to shelter owners' incomes through the use of this mechanism. (Only the thirteen clubs that were organized as partnerships or subchapter S corporations would be able, in any event, to do so.)

Table 5-4 summarizes the clubs' depreciation charges to their cash flow: As this table shows, in all four years covered the clubs had depreciation that exceeded their pretax cash flow and in the aggregate had net losses. However, these aggregate statistics present a distorted picture in which the write-offs of a few clubs greatly outweigh those of most others. To further understand this pattern, it is worth examining each of the lines in the table in more depth.

The largest amount, "Amortization of players' contracts . . . ," includes principally the amortization of signing bonuses paid to high school and college recruits. ("Net costs on contracts sold" represents a series of relatively small adjustments to account for the gains or losses from the sale of players to other clubs.) For most clubs, this item is more of an ongoing expense than a true capital item. In fact, a number of clubs using the "direct

Table 5-4
Cash Flow, Depreciation Charges, and Reported Net Income, 1974-1977

	1974		1975		1976		1977[a]	
	Dollars (000)	Percentage	Dollars (000)	Percentage	Dollars (000)	Percentage	Dollars (000)	Percentage
Cash flow before interest and taxes	8,759	100.0	10,505	100.0	13,676	100.0	18,631	100.0
Amortization of players' contracts and net costs on contracts sold	7,116	81.2	7,787	74.1	9,256	67.7	10,348	55.5
Amortization of initial roster costs	5,374	61.4	4,062	38.7	4,506	32.9	6,475	34.8
Stadium depreciation	2,636	30.1	2,523	24.0	3,140	23.0	3,046	16.3
Other depreciation	580	6.6	546	5.2	1,422	10.4	1,580	8.5
Total depreciation	15,706	179.3	14,917	142.0	18,324	134.0	21,449	115.1
Net income (loss) from operations before interest and taxes	(6,947)	(79.3)	(4,413)	(42.0)	(4,648)	(34.0)	(2,818)	(15.1)

[a]In 1974, 1975, and 1976 there were twenty-four clubs; in 1977, twenty-six.

write-off method" of accounting expense this item each year instead of capitalizing it. For a typical club, the annual amount of this amortization for player contracts and the like would range from about $150,000 to 350,000. *Three clubs reported significant amounts* in this category (that is, more than $2 million per year). Follow-up discussion with them found that the bulk of these deductions represented amortization of initial roster costs that were recorded in this category because of individual accounting methods. One of these clubs had smaller amounts in both categories.

In 1976 and 1977 (and also in 1978) there were marked increases in the "Amortization of players' contracts" caused by the rapid increase in bonuses paid to veteran players for signing multiyear contracts.

The second largest item, "Amortization of initial roster costs," is the depreciation, as discussed above, of the initial roster costs on clubs which had recently been purchased. *Except for the expansion clubs, only six clubs reported any entries in this category,* and one of those had charges for only two years, apparently having exhausted its depreciation allowance for this category. (The two expansion clubs reported entries for 1977.)

Stadium depreciation, which includes stadium improvements such as electronic scoreboards, was reported in varying amounts by most clubs.

"Other" depreciation includes such things as playing equipment, office furnishings, leasehold improvements, and the like. Such depreciation was reported in relatively small amounts by practically all clubs. Only two clubs exceeded $150,000 for such depreciation, and both of those instances occurred in a year following a change of ownership.

Thus, *most of the depreciation activity was accounted for by a relatively small number of clubs*—eight, to be exact, for the two player depreciation categories. Four clubs accounted for the bulk of the stadium depreciation.

Since players' bonuses are direct, out-of-pocket costs and have a predictable economic life, there is little basis for arguing that their amortization amounts to any form of tax shelter. Similarly, depreciation for stadium facilities, office equipment, and the like would seem to offer few, if any, opportunities for tax shelter. If a stadium or other such asset were to be sold for more than its depreciated book value, existing tax regulations provide for the recapture of taxes on any excessive depreciation that might have been claimed.

Thus, the only depreciation that arguably might constitute a form of tax shelter is the amortization of initial roster costs. And as we have observed, only a minority of clubs recorded any such amortization. Further, the Tax Reform Act of 1976 has substantially reduced the possibility for any excess of this amortization over the actual costs incurred. The act requires that both the buyer and seller in a franchise transaction agree on the portion of the purchase price that is allocated to player contracts. Since the parties presumably would deal at arm's-length on this question, the allocated amount should more closely reflect the true economic value of the contracts at the time of sale. Also, the act presumes that player contracts will represent no more than 50 percent of the purchase price, unless the purchaser can specifically show otherwise. Finally, the act provides special rules for the recapture of taxes on excessive (or excessively fast) depreciation deductions taken on player contracts when a club is sold.

In summary, most depreciation taken by baseball clubs represented the legitimate recovery of out-of-pocket capital costs for player bonuses, stadium improvements, and similar items. All deductions for the most controversial item, amortization of initial roster costs, were attributable to a very few clubs. Turnover of ownership, the principal means for exploiting any available shelter in this category, has been lower in baseball than in other professional sports. Finally, to the extent that any tax shelters were possible with sports franchises in the past, recent changes in the tax code would seem to effectively have eliminated most such possibilities.

Total Revenues of Clubs

Table 5-5 shows the distribution of clubs' total revenues from baseball operations, along with computed averages and medians for each year. Figure 5-3 depicts similar information in bar-chart form. One observation that may be made from these charts is the relatively small size of baseball clubs. By most definitions, baseball clubs were small businesses. The majority had revenues of less than $7 million, and as recently as 1976 a full quarter of them were under $5 million. There are, in fact, thousands of other local and regional enterprises which have greater revenues than the average baseball club, including many car dealerships, most community hospitals, and many other businesses. The 1974 edition of *Statistics of Income,* published by the Internal Revenue Service, reported on some 21,800 U.S. corporations that had receipts of $10 million or more. Popular comments that had characterized baseball as being big business simply do not present an accurate picture of the majority of clubs. At the grass-roots level, major-league baseball is still a group of relatively small organizations.

Another feature to observe from table 5-5 and figure 5-3 is the change that occurred between 1974 and 1977. Overall, revenues grew by 53 percent, but this change was not accomplished simply by shifting every club to the next-higher revenue category. Rather, there was a flattening of the distribution, with the bottom group (those under $5 million) dropping from eleven clubs to three and gains in several of the higher groups. The revenue gains—even after correction for the effects of expansion—appear to have taken place more among American League clubs than among National

Table 5-5
Distribution of Clubs' Total Operating Revenues,[a] 1974-1977

	Number of Clubs			
	1974	*1975*	*1976*	*1977[b]*
Less than $5 million	11	8	6	3
$5 million to $7 million	7	10	9	8
$7 million to $9 million	4	2	3	9
$9 million to $11 million	1	2	2	—
$11 million plus	1	2	4	6
	24	24	24	26

	Dollars (000)			1974-1977 Increase
Average revenues per club	5,978	6,309	7,056	8,448	41.3
Median	5,386	5,558	5,541	7,963	47.8
American League clubs combined[c]	59,725	66,519	78,648	111,212	86.2
National League clubs combined	83,745	84,906	90,704	108,446	29.5
24-Club total	$143,470	$151,425	$169,352	$219,658	53.1

Source: Tabulation from Schedule I of clubs' financial survey.

[a]These amounts include distributions which the clubs receive from the Major Leagues Central Fund (recently about $400,000 per club per year). Not included here are additional revenues which the Central Fund receives and spends directly on the clubs' behalf, principally as contributions to the players' retirement fund. In recent years, these additional revenues have ranged from $10 million to $12 million per year.

[b]1977: 26 clubs

[c]1977: 14 clubs

League clubs, and it appears that the American League thus closed a gap that had existed between itself and the National League.

As we said earlier, attendance is the largest factor affecting clubs' revenue (see figure 5-4). However, for a given attendance, revenues fell into a wide band. Thus, in looking for examples at the 1.25 million attendance level on figure 5-4, there was one club that had revenues of $4.5 million, and another, with the same attendance, having twice those revenues. Explanations for such wide variations were not readily apparent. Some clubs appear to have negotiated much better television contracts than others in similar-sized cities or under similar circumstances. The conditions of stadium leases and concessions contracts also varied considerably, with no apparent rationale in terms of city size or other circumstance.

The fitted regression lines on figure 5-4 indicate that clubs realized incremental revenues for each additional fan at the ball park, ranging from $4.19 in 1974 to $5.56 in 1977. (Not all this amount is paid directly by the fan, of course, because clubs also derive revenues from TV and radio rights and from other sources not necessarily located at the ball park.) When compared with incremental profits of $1.81 to $2.08 per additional fan, shown

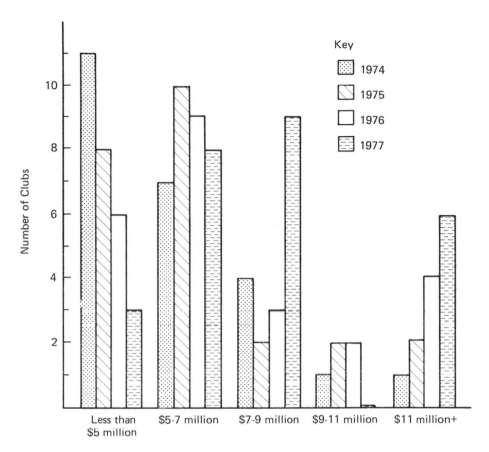

Figure 5-3. Distribution of Clubs' Total Operating Revenues, 1974-1977

earlier, this implies a long-run *incremental* profit rate of about 40 percent of revenues. Thus, *there is a strong economic incentive for clubs to increase their attendance.* Said another way, a club with a median loss of $230,000 in 1977 could have broken even by attracting another 115,000 fans to the ball park.

Sources of Revenues

We have mentioned several times the nature of baseball as a joint product and the importance of "jointness" in understanding its economics. This jointness ties clubs' sources of income together in a variety of ways. The most direct way, of course, is through the agreement to play one another,

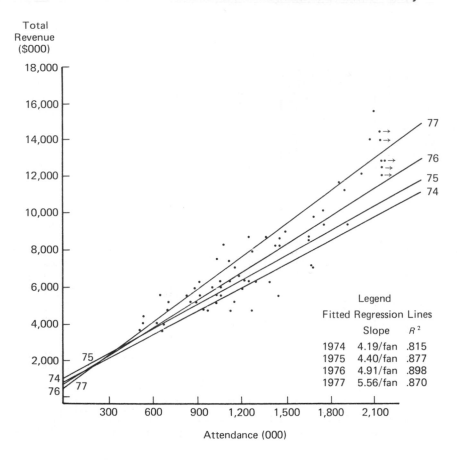

Note: Each dot represents one club one year, 1975-1977. Dots for 1974 are not shown. Arrows indicate that the dot actually occurs at a higher attendance but has been moved to 2.2 million to protect confidentiality.

Figure 5-4. Total Revenue versus Attendance, 1974-1977

which produces a contest that fans are willing to pay to watch. Having thus created (jointly) a salable product, the clubs must then decide how to divide the revenues among themselves. As a joint venture, they might, for example, divide all revenues equally among the league members. Other ways, in less of a cooperative spirit, might be to give all revenues to the winner of the game, or to let each club seek (and keep) whatever revenues it could attract from any source.

This choice is somewhat analogous to the problem of dividing prize money among contestants in a boxing match, golf tournament, or a baking contest. Without a *group* of contestants, there would be no contest and therefore no prize. Yet hardly any contest divides its prizes equally among its participants. There is a strong popular notion that the "victor takes the spoils," and most types of contests are structured to reward only the winners, allowing the majority of participants little or no compensation for their efforts.

The major-league sports fall at different points along this spectrum, ranging from near-equality to winner-take-all. Professional football is relatively equitable with television and similar revenues divided equally among all clubs and gate receipts divided 60-40 among the two participants in each game. Professional basketball is among the most inequitable, with no sharing of gate receipts or local-broadcast revenues (the home team keeps all these). Only the national-television revenues, a relatively small source for that sport, are divided equally. Baseball falls in an intermediate position. National-broadcasting revenues are divided *equally,* gate receipts are *partially* shared, and local-broadcasting revenues are kept *entirely* by the home team.

Although we do not know the origins or rationale behind these revenue-sharing arrangements, they appear to be consistent with the attendance patterns of their respective sports. Professional football games are few in number and generally are played to full stadiums. Thus, additional financial incentives to the home club would not add significantly to the number of seats sold. Baseball and basketball games, however, frequently have many empty seats, so that a strong financial incentive might very well spur a club toward greater promotion and greater efforts to win.

Figure 5-5 compares the shared and local sources of baseball clubs' revenues for 1977 (the other years showed similar patterns). In the American League, shared sources contributed about 19 percent of clubs' operating revenues. In the National League, because of a different gate-sharing agreement, the shared sources amounted to about 12 percent. Thus, in 1977 the average American League club received about $1.5 million, and the average National League club received about $1.1 million, in addition to whatever local revenues it could generate.[3] Obviously, for clubs in smaller cities and especially for those clubs whose total revenues were $5 million or less, these shared sources provided an important base of revenue on which to build.

At the same time, local sources still accounted for the bulk of clubs' direct revenues: 81 percent in the American League and 88 percent in the National League. Thus, clubs still had a strong economic incentive for improving their own fortunes. As we saw in chapter 3, there are two principal ways a club can attract more fans: by *winning* more games (and especially by being a contender for first place) and by increasing its *marketing and promotion* activities.

The first strategy works at least partly at the *expense* of fellow league members, since it means that some of them must *lose* more games and thus

	American League (14 Clubs)		National League (12 Clubs)		Major-League Baseball	
	$ 000	% of AL Revenue	$ 000	% of NL Revenue	$ 000	% of Total
Local Sources						
Home Game Receipts	57,931	52.1	64,242	59.2	122,173	50.9
Local TV and Radio	11,900	10.7	12,917	11.9	24,817	10.3
Concessions	18,508	16.6	15,434	14.2	33,942	14.1
Participants: Proceeds of World Series and League Championship Series	1,546	1.4	2,269	2.1	3,815	1.6
Other Local Sources	466	.4	534	.5	1,000	.4
Subtotal — Local Sources	90,351	81.2	95,396	88.0	185,747	77.3
Joint Sources						
Away Game Receipts	14,892	13.4	6,880	6.3	21,772	9.1
Major League Central Fund Distributions to Clubs	5,430	4.9	5,630	5.2	11,060	4.6
World Series and L.C.S. Distribution to Clubs	540	.5	540	.5	1,000	.4
Subtotal — Joint Sources	20,862	18.8	13,050	12.0	33,912	14.1
Joint Revenues Centrally Spent					20,545	8.6
Clubs' Total Operating Revenues / Grand Total	111,212	100.0	108,446	100.0	240,203	100.0

Joint Revenues Centrally Spent
+ • Major League Central Fund $11,317
  • League Championship Series and World Series $4,454
  • Leagues' Share of Gate Receipts $4,774

(Paid for Players Benefit Trust, umpires and their expenses, Office of the Commissioner, League offices, Player Relations Committee, and other joint expenses)

Figure 5-5. Summary of Clubs' Individual and Joint Revenue Sources, 1977

Source: Most figures were tabulated from Schedule II of the clubs' financial survey for 1977. Centrally spent figures were derived from the sources used for those same items in figure 4-3.

Note: Details may not add to totals because of rounding.

lose fan interest and revenues. The second strategy works to the *benefit* of fellow league members by increasing the total gate receipts to be shared. We found in our field interviews and in observing clubs' behavior that some clubs were substantially more aggressive than others in their marketing and promotion efforts. Since there is a leaguewide interest in improving the marketing effectiveness of *all* clubs, this would seem to be yet another opportunity for joint agreement and joint action.

As the cost of players' salaries increases, there is likely to be increasing pressure for clubs to recognize their mutual interest in better *local* marketing as a strategy for enlarging all clubs' revenues.

Components of Revenues

Figure 5-5 indicates the major components of clubs' local sources of revenues, with home gate receipts representing more than half of total revenues and concessions and local broadcasting together accounting for another one-fourth of revenues. The amounts of each of these items varied greatly among clubs, as shown graphically in figures 5-6 and 5-7. Home game receipts followed a skewed distribution similar to clubs' total revenues, with most clubs clustered toward the lower end of the range. This pattern was very similar to the clubs' attendance pattern, as would be expected.

Concession revenues were not as closely related to attendance (see figure 5-7). The wide range in concession revenues for a given attendance arose, in part, from different concessions and concession arrangements at the different ball parks. Some parks had stadium clubs, others did not. Some clubs gave up all or part of their concession revenues in return for a lower stadium rent. On the average, clubs averaged about $0.78 in concession revenues per fan over the four years.

Local broadcasting yielded an unexpected pattern of revenues, with some clubs in the largest cities earning less than many clubs with smaller markets. No one with whom we spoke could explain this pattern, although some speculated that big-city television stations might have more competition (and hence lower ratings) than stations in smaller markets. However, the absence of higher revenues is generally consistent with the attendance studies presented in chapter 4. There, too, in interest baseball in large cities fell below the levels one might expect on the basis of attendance in smaller cities.

General and Administrative Expense

Some commentators have speculated that baseball owners might disguise their club profits in the form of large salaries for themselves, high living on

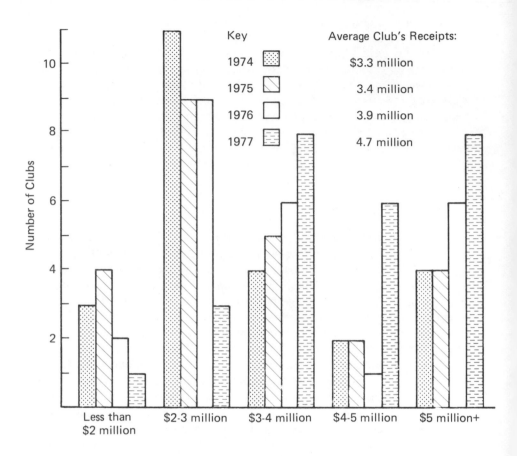

Source: Tabulated from Schedule I of clubs' financial survey.

Figure 5-6. Distribution of Regular-Season Home-Game Receipts (Net of League Share and Visiting-Club Shares), 1974-1977

expense accounts, and other types of spending which are charged to "club administration."

Our financial survey did not ask for owner's salaries or their charges to club expense accounts, but it did obtain a rather detailed breakdown of clubs' general and administrative expenses (see Appendixes C and D). Such expenses, above a certain minimum of about $1.0 million per year, varied in close relation to the total revenues of the club (see figure 5-8).

Overall, administrative expenses ranged between 13.8 and 14.5 percent of clubs' total revenues during the four years. Such a level may appear high in comparison with, say, a manufacturing enterprise, where the typical

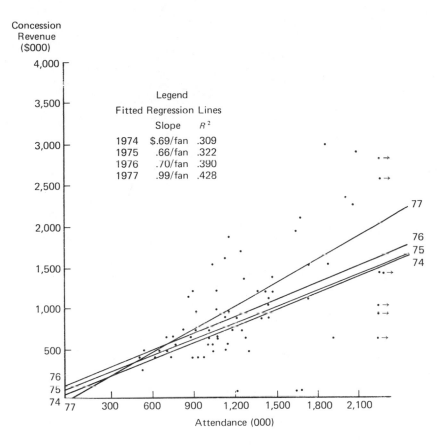

Concession
Revenue
($000)

Legend

Fitted Regression Lines

	Slope	R^2
1974	$.69/fan	.309
1975	.66/fan	.322
1976	.70/fan	.390
1977	.99/fan	.428

Attendance (000)

Note: Each dot represents one club one year, 1975-1977. Dots for 1974 are not shown. Arrows indicate that the dot actually occurs at a higher attendance but has been moved to 2.2 million to protect confidentiality.

Figure 5-7. Concession Revenues versus Attendance, 1974-1977

range might be 5 to 10 percent of sales. However, we think this is not a meaningful comparison, because in manufacturing firms or other large organizations, the product is created by a large number of relatively unskilled workers and by capital equipment. A more appropriate comparison, we believe, would be with law firms, architectural firms, group medical practices, consulting firms, and similar types of organizations in which the product is generated by a small number of highly paid professionals. In such enterprises, administrative expenses often run to as much as one-quarter of total revenues.

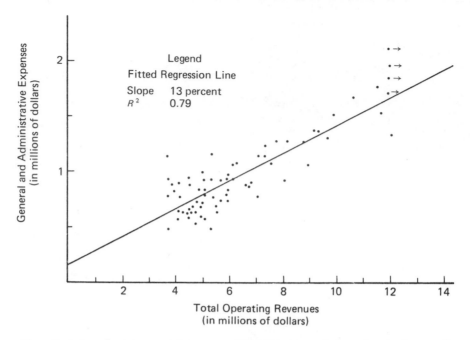

Note: Each dot represents one club one year, 1974-1976. Arrows indicate that the dot actually occurs at a higher total operating revenue but has been moved to $12 million to protect confidentiality.

Figure 5-8. General and Administrative Expenses versus Total Operating Revenues for All Baseball Clubs, 1974-1976

Summary

Several key points stand out in the analysis of clubs' financial performance during the years surveyed:

1. Most clubs were unprofitable. Only a handful made money. Also, a very few clubs (not the same ones) accounted for the bulk of depreciation.

2. Attendance was the primary factor that determined revenues and earnings. Clubs' financial success depended heavily on the fan at the ball park. (Attendance also was closely related to stadium and administrative expenses.)

3. Clubs showed great variability, even for a given attendance, in their patterns of revenues. This variability appears to be related to differences in stadium leases, broadcasting arrangements, and ticket prices. Expenses also showed a wide range of variation, suggesting that there is no clear-cut minimum cost of operation.

4. Clubs needed an attendance of almost 1 million (1974-1976) to 1.2 million (1977) fans to cover basic costs, although this, too, showed considerable range of variation, with some clubs losing money on higher attendance and some being profitable at lower levels.

These observations are generally consistent with the characteristics of baseball discussed in chapter 3. Except for a very few clubs, profits in relation to revenues, or in relation to the likely asset value of a club, were well below the ranges found in most business enterprises. It is also clear that financial results depended strongly on attendance, which in turn depended on team performance. The financial balancing mechanisms for the leagues, of gate sharing and joint sale of national-broadcasting rights, provide each club with dependable sources of outside income, but the dominant factor remains the club's own development of its local market.

Notes

1. U.S. Congress, House, Select Committee on Professional Sports, *Final Report* (Washington: USGPO, 1976), p. 591.

2. The 1965 data are not precisely comparable because they include interest expense and income from investments. Based on current experience from such items, the 1965 figures probably should be increased by about 3 to 8 percent to get an estimate of income from baseball operations only. These figures can vary significantly depending on how recently the club changed ownership.

3. In addition to these club revenues, the Major Leagues Central Fund and other joint enterprises received revenues and spent them jointly on behalf of the clubs, for example, for administrative expenses of the commissioner's office or contributions to the Players Benefit Trust. In aggregate, these expenditures amounted to about $20.5 million for the 1977 season.

6

Policy Implications: Summary and Conclusions

Major-league baseball—in fact, the professional sports industry in general—holds a certain fascination for students of public policy toward business. The source of this fascination is rooted in what has come to be called the baseball "anomaly." Put simply, this term signifies a concept that can best be captured in the following syllogism:

Major premise: The nation's antitrust laws apply to all private enterprise.

Minor premise: Major-league baseball is private enterprise.

Anomaly: The antitrust laws do *not* apply to major-league baseball.

To elaborate, our antitrust laws prohibit the improper accumulation or exercise of undue market power and collective arrangements among ostensibly competing businesses—especially cooperative agreements that limit their independent competitive actions, such as those that fix price, allocate sales territories, limit output, or restrict entry. In apparent contrast, the three basic institutional arrangements governing the conduct of major-league baseball are control over entry of new franchises into a league, the territorial exclusivity of league franchises, and player-control arrangements such as league rules pertaining to the drafting of new players and the reserve clause. At first blush, then, it appears that those restraining agreements which the antitrust laws forbid in other businesses are permitted in major-league baseball by virtue of its antitrust immunities.

The association of club franchises into a league, each binding itself to abide by league rules, has led some who have studied these arrangements to conclude that leagues function as cartels. For example, Noll states that a "professional sports league is essentially a cartel with the purpose of restricting competition and dividing markets among firms in the industry."[1] No one would deny that collective control over such matters as entry, market territory, and competition for an essential factor of production is numbered among the preoccupations of cartelized industries. But to conclude uncritically from such surface similarities that the American and National Leagues function as conventional cartels is to ignore the peculiar features of league sports and the motivational forces behind cartel practices.

Formal cartels have traditionally been defined as "compacts providing administrative machinery for regulating output, sharing markets and fixing prices."[2] In most cartelized industries, individual members can increase output independently of their rivals with relatively low incremental costs. Therefore, without an agreement, each producer has a strong incentive to gain additional business at the expense of its rivals by cutting price. The objective of the cartel is to ensure that such independent action, which would eventually make all members of the industry worse off, does not occur.

It is clear that the professional baseball leagues do not exist in order to carry out these traditional cartel functions. The rules and regulations governing the clubs comprising the league are essential to the *creation* of the league as an *entity* and have virtually nothing to do with the pricing policies of individual clubs.

In fact, it has been proposed that the league is the relevant unit for economic analysis of the sports industry, and that this proposition holds equal validity for the Ivy League, the Southwest Conference, and the Big Ten as it does for the American and National Baseball Leagues.[3] The league stages a championship season of games among a given number of contesting clubs according to common rules. This "product" is possible only through the cooperative efforts of the league members. League members must necessarily enter into agreements in order to establish the common rules, organize a season of games, and maintain a balance between the clubs' incentives (economic and otherwise) to win and the reasonable degree of competitive strength among contestants needed for close, exciting games. The important *economic* competition is not *among* the contestants but between the whole league and other forms of entertainment. It follows from this proposition that the leagues, as entities, could not continue in their present form if baseball were subject, in a narrow sense, to antitrust liabilities. The sport would be subject to immense uncertainties and constant legal challenge. In short, the objective of the cooperative agreements that govern the clubs constituting a league is not to constrain the economic competition among them, but rather to create the league as a joint venture that "produces" baseball during a season of play. Without such rules of conduct as those that currently govern league members, or similar rules that would serve the same purposes, leagues would not exist.

We confront, then, two alternative and conflicting hypotheses concerning means by which major-league baseball is conducted; the system of rules and regulations that league members abide by equates the leagues with conventional cartels, or, alternatively, since the provisions of a corporate charter are necessary to a corporation, they are necessary for the creation of a league as an entity. A third and fundamentally different possible interpretation of professional baseball is that the clubs should not be analyzed as ordinary profit-seeking enterprises. Under this hypothesis, the incentives that govern their conduct are more akin to those associated with the Boston Symphony or the Philadelphia Philharmonic than to those associated with General Motors. Thus, according to this interpretation, baseball for some club owners is an interesting sideline; for others, it is a symbol of community pride; for still others, it is a form of art to be patronized. A satisfactory economic goal is simply to cover expenses or to make a small profit. The real objective, however, is to build the best team in the country and to bring home pennants, excitement, fame, and glory for the hometown.

If this interpretation is valid, it follows that a narrowly constructed application of antitrust liabilities that would result in increasing baseball's costs might tip the balance to the point where some owners would no longer choose to continue. Whether new owners could be found who were willing to accept the added cost is a matter of conjecture. If such an interpretation were valid, the likely result, we believe, would be a restriction in the number of teams or, if the market would bear it, a considerable rise in ticket prices and/or a lowering of average player salaries.

In the analysis that follows, these hypotheses are tested against the factual evidence presented in the earlier chapters. The analysis focuses particularly on the issues of entry, players' contracts, and profitability. Since these issues, along with the territorial exclusivity of club franchises, give rise to the baseball "anomaly," their analysis provides a foundation for estimating the possible consequences of eliminating the anomaly, that is, for formulating an informed judgment as to what might happen if baseball's structural arrangements were found to be in violation of antitrust laws and were stricken down.

Financial Performance

Over the 1974-1978 period for which financial data are available on all the major-league baseball clubs, almost two out of every three clubs operated at a loss. In a typical year, only one or two clubs earned a before-tax profit in excess of $2 million. In no year did the two leagues, combined, earn a profit, although the attendance successes of 1978 managed to reduce the aggregate loss to $34,000.[4]

This record of financial performance casts serious doubt on the cartel hypothesis. First, profits for the industry are generally negative, and there are no known "ordinary" industries, much less cartels, in which the average firm consistently loses money. Furthermore, baseball clubs' profits are *highly variable*, depending strongly on team performance. Both of these phenomena are entirely inconsistent with normal cartel performance. The expected result of a cartel's successful restraint on entry and control of players' salaries would be a reasonably satisfactory industry profit record—or at least a reduction in the losses of the cartels' more poorly performing members. Neither of these results was found. Nor do the financial data support the contention of some critics that there were indeed profits but that somehow they have been hidden in the form of tax shelters, capital gains, or excessive overhead expenses. Even if all depreciation were considered a profit, baseball clubs still would not have been economically attractive investments.

It may be argued that the lack of profits alone is not conclusive evidence that leagues do not function as cartels. For example, it may be the case that the total revenues fall short of total cost for the baseball industry as a whole, even at the cartel price. However, this would imply that the prices are, in fact, fixed by the league and that clubs have expanded to the point of excess capacity. As the factual data presented in this book clearly show, the league does not fix the prices charged by the individual clubs, and expansion to the point of persistent excess capacity would be inconsistent with rational cartel behavior.

Alternatively, it may be argued that clubs simply are not managed efficiently or that club owners intentionally or unintentionally engage in managerial practices that understate true profits—for example, they hide profits in expense accounts, in the payment of excessive salaries to management, or by other accounting manipulations. Our financial analysis of the industry provides no reason to conclude that the accounting standards used by major-league clubs differ to any substantial degree from those used by business generally. Administrative expenses, above a certain minimum, tended to rise in direct proportion to total revenues. The level of these expenses, while higher than that of a manufacturing business, was in line with the administrative expenses of many professional service organizations, such as in the areas of education, health care, financial services, and the performing arts.

Our field studies of baseball club owners and managers revealed considerable variation in the quality and aggressiveness of management. Some clubs were quite energetic and innovative in such areas as promoting home games and developing budgets and cost controls; others demonstrated a lower degree of expertise in these operations. On balance, we conclude that mismanagement is not a sufficient explanation for the clubs' low profits.

The central flaw in the cartel hypothesis, however, is that it fails to distinguish between the necessity for club cooperation which is required for a league to exist (indeed, for a season's schedule of games to be played) and the voluntary association of otherwise independent companies which is necessary for them to function as a cartel. Accordingly, it overlooks the inescapable joint financial interests of members of a league sport. On the matter of entry, for example, every league member is forced to play the new entrant, whether it wants to or not. There is no "market" for opponents in, say, Atlanta; the requirement is to play exactly eighty-one away games per season, whether the attendance is good or not. If attendance is low, as it was for several years, a direct loss of revenue is imposed on the visiting teams. (See the discussion in chapter 3.) In a league schedule there is no opportunity for teams to redeploy their resources to more profitable and exciting contests.

This peculiar feature of competitive league sports, which is often described as the "inverted joint product" nature of the output, explains why entry into a league of necessity requires the consent of existing league members. Unlike with most businesses, a prospective entrant into a baseball league cannot assemble the requisite capital, workforce, and supporting resources and begin immediately to produce baseball games. Even for the production of a single game, the prospective entrant must enter into an agreement with another team; to enter a league and participate in a season schedule obviously requires the consent of those teams that constitute the league.

Furthermore, since the total number of games each team plays in a given season is fixed, the entry of an additional team into a league does not increase a club's total number of games (that is, the existing clubs' total output); it merely alters the geographical distribution of the games. For example, when the Toronto Blue Jays and the Seattle Mariners were admitted to the American League in 1977, the result was that older league members such as the Boston Red Sox played fewer games with such established rivals as New York, Baltimore, Detroit, and Cleveland, playing instead with Toronto and Seattle who were unknown quantities to the fans. Again, unlike with conventional cartels, restrictions on entry in major-league baseball are not for the purposes of restricting output—the total output of games for each of the clubs is determined by the number of playing days in the season.

Stated somewhat differently, the entry of new teams into a league leaves the output in the relevant home markets unchanged, set at eighty-one games per season under present schedules. However, new entrants do add new markets, requiring existing league members to reallocate some of their away games from old markets to new markets. It is important to note, however, that these new markets are distinctive markets of their own and are not in competition for attendance with other markets. It is highly unlikely that an *existing* club would logically reason that it would have to charge a lower price to accommodate an increase in output with the addition of a new entrant to its league.[5]

It is equally obvious that baseball leagues do not serve the function most often associated with cartels, namely, the setting of the prices charged by league members. Analysis of ticket prices for the twenty-six clubs constituting the two major leagues for the 1955, 1965, 1970, 1975, and 1978 seasons shows a wide variation among the clubs as a whole and among clubs in each league. For example, in 1978 bleacher seats in the American League ranged from $1.00 for Baltimore and Cleveland to a high of $2.50 for Boston; the highest-priced seats in the ball park ranged from $4.00 for the California Angels to $7.00 for the Kansas City Royals. It is clear from the data and from our field studies that individual clubs act independently in setting their admission prices and in arriving at their contractual terms for local broadcasting. This independence takes on added significance in view of the interdependence of clubs in producing games. Since in the course of a baseball season each club must cooperate with all the other clubs in its league in producing its eighty-one home games, and since visiting teams share in the gate receipts of the game they help produce, we might logically expect to find some evidence of cooperative leaguewide pricing. The persuasive evidence to the contrary is quite inconsistent with the cartel hypothesis.

When the special characteristics of a league sport are assessed against the nonfinancial motivations of some owners, the poor financial performance is easier to understand. Although the average team incurs a loss for participating in the race, there is a prize in the form of higher attendance at (and participation in) league play-offs and the World Series for teams that perform well. (Even this prize, however, is shared to some extent with other members of the league.) Losing teams can expect to lose money, despite the sharing of certain league revenues. However, the presence of even a few owners who are willing to accept losses or low profits tends to lower the financial performance of all league members.

As the analysis has shown, fan interest in league sports depends heavily on relatively evenly matched teams. If a few owners try to buy up the top players at high salaries, one of two outcomes is possible:

1. Other teams may do nothing, in which case the games become more one-sided and attendance suffers.
2. Other teams must spend at similar levels and accept similar financial results.

This phenomenon has, in fact, become very evident in the bidding for veteran and free-agent players that began in 1976. A few clubs, such as the New York Yankees, the California Angels, and the Philadelphia Phillies, committed much larger sums to players' contracts than did most of the other clubs—more than ten times the spending of some. Consistent with earlier spending patterns, the less well-heeled clubs sharply increased their spending in an effort to catch up, but they still did not keep pace.

As a recent study of player movements concluded, "the effective termination of the reserve clause for veteran players in 1976 has been followed by a series of free agent transactions which have on balance clearly strengthened [the higher spending] teams."[6]

Entry of New Franchises

Under the present American League constitution, adding a new franchise or moving an existing one requires a three-fourths vote of the league members. The National League requires a unanimous vote to expand the league and a three-fourths vote to relocate an existing member. Both leagues also grant each member an exclusive territory within a specified distance.[7] Further, in past expansions, both leagues have required the payment of substantial entry fees, either as outright payments or as compensation for players drafted from existing clubs.

While these restrictions would appear to support the cartel hypothesis, they are nevertheless necessary in order to attain important league objectives such as a championship season of games, a standard set of playing rules, and evenly matched games, which the baseball public generally considers desirable. The relevant issue therefore, is not whether they are restrictive but, in view of the results obtained, whether they are more restrictive than they need be in order to obtain the desired objectives.

League Concerns

An objective of high priority to the leagues is *continuity and stability*. Clearly some of the restrictions governing franchises are necessary from a standpoint of scheduling.[8] Also, baseball fans place great value on being able to compare team performance and player averages against the records of prior years.[9] Thus, the leagues have an interest in ensuring that new clubs have at least a reasonable chance of lasting success.

A second objective is maximum attendance. Adding new teams to the schedule reduces the number of times that old, established rivals can play each other, and attendance suffers accordingly. We pointed earlier to the example of the Boston Red Sox, who in early-season games at Fenway Park drew about 19,000 fewer fans per game for a Toronto series than for a Detroit Tigers series. Past experience has shown that it takes several years—seldom less than five—for an expansion team to make its way up from the lowest league standings. During this start-up period, the team is likely to be a below-average draw for its fellow league members.

In effect, then, each club makes an investment in a new entrant. The entry fees paid by a new entrant are generally only a partial compensation for this investment. In the event some club is failing, this investment may become quite real and direct for the others. Certainly no cartel would seek to maintain competitive production capacity in this way. Although not written into league agreements, in the past leagues have stepped in and helped to support a failing club until new ownership could be found for the floundering franchise, a practice that sharply distinguishes baseball clubs from other enterprises. Again, it underscores the league's direct economic interest in ensuring the success of new entrants.

Leagues are also concerned that stadium leases are financially viable. It has become a common practice in the United States for public agencies to finance the construction of sports stadia.[10] Their costs are then recovered through annual lease payments from the teams.[11] If a new team fails or moves to another city, the taxpayers are left holding a facility that has very limited use and may not be viable without baseball revenues. Major legal actions in Milwaukee, San Diego, Seattle, and more recently Oakland testify to the resentment that occurs when a poorly performing team seeks to leave a publicly financed stadium. To avoid ill will, to say nothing of costly lawsuits, leagues have a vital interest in limiting entry to teams that have good prospects for long-term success. However, this interest springs from financial and public-confidence considerations completely unrelated to conventional cartel objectives.

Finally, leagues are concerned about controlling factors that might lead to dilution of the quality of the game. If, as has been contended, there is a limited supply of good baseball players, further expansion of the leagues can be accomplished only by adding players who are considered to be of lower caliber. While it cannot be empirically determined whether such a limit exists, the possibility of its existence enhances the importance of the concern over league balance. Our analysis has shown the close link among attendance, profits, and team performance. A new entrant must have sufficient financial resources to recruit and develop a competitive team and to sustain itself for several years of start-up losses. Without such staying power, the team is almost doomed to a cellar-dwelling, marginal existence, to the detriment of the quality of the game that inevitably results from league imbalance.

Experience with Entry

Ten teams have been added to major-league baseball since 1961, and there is reason to believe that several of the existing clubs are operating on the margin of existence. The distribution of club profits, with a number of the clubs incurring repeated losses, and the wide variation in player payrolls, with the poorer clubs spending much less than the average, suggests that several face substantial risk of insolvency or outright failure. This risk is not new to major-league history. Over the years there have been several instances of clubs that have reached the verge of bankruptcy and have been propped up by the leagues, sold at substantial losses, or forced to relocate in order to remain alive as a franchise. Economic failure under the standards applied to business in general has been just as real in baseball as it has been in other types of enterprise. However, it is the absence of "exits" from the industry in the form of closed franchises that gives baseball its unusual characteristics. In part, this preservation of franchises can be explained in terms of the leagues' concerns with stability and balance. Leagues have helped weak clubs weather rough times and have assisted them in finding new owners. But this perseverence is also partly attributable to the willingness of some individuals or local business groups to give it a try despite the risks—to take over a franchise out of motives other than just the prospects for profit.

Options for Baseball

The rules governing entry—particularly the National League's unanimity rule—often have been criticized as undue restraints on entry and, at least by inference, as anticompetitive. In the words of Congressman Horton, ". . . this is the thing I have the most problem with on the antitrust immunity—is the fact that in one league they have to have a unanimous decision with regard to some very vital matters that affect the structure of baseball."[12] By application of the conventional standards of workable competition, such control over new entry would be anticompetitive. However, as pointed out at virtually every turn in this book, major-league baseball is not a conventional industry. Unlike other industries, the entry of a new team in a city where none now exists does not enhance competition for "consumers" of baseball—the fans. Moreover, the entry of a new club into either of the major leagues requires that all the existing clubs join with it to jointly produce the season's schedule of games. It is difficult to contemplate a workable system for accommodating the addition of a new club that did not require the consent of those teams on whose cooperation the new club must inevitably rely. Hence the entry of new clubs into a league poses a dilemma: to require the consent of all the existing clubs raises the issue of undue restrictions on entry; not to require such consent raises the issue of coercion—the forcing of at least some clubs to alter their schedules, their travel, and all the complicated arrangements involved in league participation, against their will.

This dilemma arises out of the special and peculiar features of major-league baseball, namely, the clubs comprising a league do not compete with each other in the usual product-market sense. A game played in Detroit does not compete for fans with a game played in Boston. However, clubs *do* compete with each other for players. To modify the existing rules governing entry might have the effect of increasing the demand for players and therefore the bargaining power of players in dealing with club owners. In view of the rapidly rising salaries of players in recent years and the erosion of the reserve system, it is not clear that this additional bargaining power is needed. Judgment of this matter clearly requires further study. For now, we can only remind those who manage the business aspects of baseball that the rules governing entry into a league are of public concern and hence are an issue they should seriously address.

Territorial Limits

Of all the elements of baseball league operations that are governed by agreed-upon rules, the exclusive territorial privileges that are granted to league members most closely resemble a feature generally associated with conventional cartel activity. The National League grants territorial exclusivity to its clubs within the city limits of their home cities and within a 10-mile area extending in all directions from the city limits, while in the American League establishment of a club within 100 miles of an existing club requires the consent of the latter. The league rules are especially restrictive only for the special cases of a third team in cities with a population of at least 2.4 million or a second team in cities of smaller size. Only New York has had a history of three teams, and in spite of the piquant "subway series" in the 1947-1957 period, the Giants in two World Series between 1950 and 1957 were drawing less than 600,000 in attendance per year when they moved to San Francisco in 1959. Even the redoubtable Brooklyn Dodgers had experienced a gradual decline in attendance of from over 1.5 million per year in the late 1940s to less than 1 million in four of the six years prior to their move to Los Angeles. And as described earlier, the attendance records of the "second" teams in most of the cities that once were two-team cities strongly suggest that their financial viability depended heavily on their moving to more promising cities. The annual attendance for the Boston Braves, St. Louis Browns, and Philadelphia Athletics had dwindled to a few hundred thousand prior to their respective moves to what they hoped would be greener pastures.

All five of these moves brought large metropolitan areas their first major-league franchises, yet still allowed the cities that were left behind access to major-league baseball. And in greatly increasing the availability of baseball to the national population, the moves more than likely also added to the public welfare.

With respect to *inter*league moves, a club of one league may be located in a city already occupied by the other league, provided its ball park is at least 5 miles distant from the park of the preexisting club. However, such entry requires a three-quarters vote of the preexisting league for cities with a population of less than 2.4 million. No consent is necessary in the case of the cities of larger size. Similarly, the leagues grant each club an exclusive right to broadcast its own games (both home and away) within its own home territory, which is defined as the area within a 50-mile radius of its ball park. While the clubs are free to a degree to broadcast their own home games elsewhere in the country, as a matter of actual practice they have generally limited broadcasts and telecasts to that area which would normally be regarded as their regional trade territory and from which they could expect to attract fans to their park.

While the league and its constituent clubs obviously have a legitimate interest in limiting club franchises to those population centers that can provide the critical mass required for long-run financial viability, there is no way of demonstrating that those particular restrictions that have been agreed upon are the best means to serve the league objectives of stability, equality of teams, or the quality of the game.

To be sure, there is little, if any, factual evidence that the existing rules governing their franchises have denied entry to prospectively viable clubs. The history of multiteam cities would suggest that the rules governing territorial exclusivity have not prevented, to any substantial degree, the entry of new franchises into metropolitan areas already served by a major-league club; the economic disincentive to enter such cities would seldom require that the rules be exercised. The more recent creation of the multiclub metropolitan areas of San Diego-Anaheim-Los Angeles and San Francisco-Oakland is further evidence that the rules do not preclude entry when the economic incentives to enter are sufficiently strong. Moreover, territorial exclusivity is not unique to major-league baseball franchises. In many lines of business a franchise is granted territorial exclusivity on the grounds that it alone can provide sufficient incentive for the required investment in capital, market development, and promotion. For the most part, territories are apportioned on such economic bases as population, the number of potential customers and the cost of serving them, and so on.

We would not predict, as some have, that as a result of less restrictive rules, large cities such as New York and Los Angeles might end up with four or five teams. Our studies show that per capita baseball attendance declines sharply with increasing city size, whether the city has one team or two. As pointed out above, the historical record of two-team cities such as Boston, Philadelphia, St. Louis, and San Francisco-Oakland would suggest that economic considerations, rather than the league rules, have been the main deterrent to multiteam cities. The experience of clubs in two-team cities in other sports tends to corroborate this conclusion. This attendance record has often been explained in terms of people's lifestyles, a wider range of alternative entertainment, and logistical problems such as difficulties of transportation and parking. Even if the rules governing entry were to be relaxed, these economic barriers to entry would remain and would probably constrain the two major leagues to approximately their present number and geographical distribution of clubs.

Player Contracting

The 1976 collective-bargaining agreement and the events leading up to it have resulted in greatly increased compensation for many players. Those who have tended to view the leagues as cartels would offer this as evidence confirming that the reserve system, in its previous form, was an undue exercise of monopoly power by baseball clubs. But an equally plausible hypothesis is that the 1976 agreement unleashed the monopoly power of star players. The bidding contest that ensued has created a situation much like previous league wars. If history is any guide, the skyrocketing salaries and intensified player mobility will lead ultimately to the failure of weaker clubs or to some type of mechanism to realign the playing strengths among clubs.

Underlying the instability resulting from the bidding war is the fact that star players are unique and limited. A Reggie Jackson, a Ron Guidry, or a Pete Rose has few, if any, ready substitutes. This gives each star enormous bargaining power and, coupled with the willingness of some owners to accept the prospects of little or no returns, collectively leads to uneconomic investments. Other clubs are faced with a choice of meeting the high salary offers or losing their better players, and the whole scale of player costs rises, leading to increased losses or reduced profits for a larger number of clubs.

This pattern has occurred often in league wars in baseball and other sports and has repeated itself in the post-1976 free-agent bidding. The possible outcomes are fairly predictable:

1. Owners continue to sustain losses or reduced profitability or sell to new owners willing to do so.
2. Clubs cover the added costs by reducing other expenses or by increasing revenues through exploiting the controversy and glamour surrounding the highly paid players.
3. The weaker clubs fail, releasing their players into the bidding competition and thereby exerting a dampening effect on salaries.
4. Significant numbers of new, high-quality players are attracted into baseball by the high salaries.
5. Some new balancing mechanism, acceptable to the players' union, is devised.

In past league wars, outcomes 2 and 3 have been the most frequent results, leading ultimately to some form of truce involving mutual restraint. Because of the long training time and uncertainty in predicting success, it is doubtful that the present instability will be remedied by an increase in the supply of high-quality players.

In the past, baseball clubs have put forth two justifications for the reserve system: (1) it allowed them to recoup their investment in recruiting and training players, and (2) it supported competitive balance by preventing the wealthiest clubs from buying all the good players. Both arguments would seem to have merit. In many respects, the present six-year reserve requirement, after which a player then becomes a free agent, is analogous to the protection given the holder of a patent. It creates an incentive for clubs to invest in a highly uncertain venture (the new player) by providing a time to reap the benefits if the player develops into one of major-league quality. Whether six years is the optimum period to recoup the outlays on player development may be subject to debate, but the *principle* has been an accepted tenet of our national economic policy since the adoption of the patent system and evidently has been accepted by the players' union in the existing contract.

On the question of competitive balance, the empirical research of others indicates that the reserve system, in its earlier form, did tend (partially) to balance teams' strengths.[13] As chapter 5 showed, the free-agent bidding has indeed further *unbalanced* the teams' payroll spending, in addition to raising the overall levels of spending.

Antitrust Exemption Reexamined

The analysis presented in earlier chapters, the essential features of which have been drawn together above, has led to the inescapable conclusion that conventional antitrust analysis is fundamentally inapplicable to major-league baseball clubs as individual entities. A comprehensive system of agreements binding clubs to certain rules, schedules, formulas for division of joint-product revenues, and so on are essential to the functioning of a league. In virtually all its aspects except the acquisition of players and the actual playing of the games themselves, major-league baseball is essentially a cooperative rather than a competitive enterprise. Individual clubs do not compete with each other for business; on the contrary, they must rely on other teams to join with them to produce an output—the game. This cooperation, however, is not to be confused with those collusive agreements that establish cartels. Nor is it concerned with restricting output or setting price; it is simply a necessary concomitant of a league's existence.

Moreover, none of the usual commercial indices of monopoly provide support for the hypothesis that the major leagues operate as business cartels. In a typical year, most of the clubs constituting a league are likely to sustain losses; the combined net income of all clubs making up the two major leagues has been negative in virtually every year covered in our financial analysis. Individual clubs have complete independence with regard to their pricing of admission and concessions and with respect to the terms they negotiate with the media for local broadcasting. The sale of national-broadcasting rights is already exempted by Congress from the antitrust laws. The application of antitrust doctrine to strike down existing practices therefore would not eliminate price coordination and monopoly profits (the usual social costs of cartels) because there simply are none of these costs to eliminate. Nor would it be likely to benefit the baseball public in the form of reduced ticket prices or more franchises, because these factors are already determined principally by economic considerations, not by league rules.

Finally, collective arrangements among clubs, which are embodied in league rules that in the past have been the major target of antitrust criticism, recently have been substantially modified to the point that antitrust remedies would no longer be applicable—even in the absence of baseball's special immunity. The growth in strength of the Major League Baseball Players Association has made player salaries and reserve provisions now a matter of collective bargaining.

Since owner-player relations are now governed by the process of collective bargaining, entry into the leagues and the territorial exclusivity of club franchises are the principal remaining issues that the antitrust laws might address. However, total freedom of entry, which antitrust laws are designed to ensure in other contexts, would disrupt the major leagues as they have functioned historically (including the value of team standings and championships). This is clearly a situation that is not likely to receive the popular support of the baseball public, and it has not been advanced as a serious proposal even by baseball's strongest critics. Imposing antitrust laws on the industry would nevertheless burden the courts with deciding on a case-by-case basis the reasonableness of the leagues' rules governing entry and with disposing of a potential stream of lawsuits brought by any group seeking a major-league franchise.

There remains to be considered the league rule providing for the reverse-order draft of new recruits. Presumably, since this rule is a product of an agreement among league members, it could be subject to challenge were baseball to lose its antitrust immunity. If the draft were eliminated, baseball would very likely revert to the "bonus baby" system that prevailed in earlier days, with the highest-spending clubs getting the most promising players. Again, this is a result that is likely to be unpopular with baseball fans. Assuming some form of draft were preserved (say, by special legislation), clubs probably would turn to multiyear contracts with their minor-league players as they have with major-league players. Such an arrangement would be conceptually equivalent to the current practice in which players are guaranteed a standard minimum salary scale and negotiations take place over additional compensation. Thus, assuming some type of reverse-order draft, a device used by virtually all professional sports, minor-league player costs may not be significantly affected by a change in baseball's antitrust status. Given the high priority that the baseball public places on team balance, the present drafting system would hardly warrant extending the antitrust laws to baseball.

There would appear to be more efficacious policy solutions to the unresolved issues surrounding major-league baseball than the one proposed—that of opening up the sport to a deluge of antitrust litigation. No one would deny that major-league baseball is, to borrow a phrase from regulatory language, "affected with a public interest." The public, however, because of baseball's inherent cooperative characteristics, cannot depend on the economic marketplace to regulate competition among clubs. Nonetheless, the public deserves to know how the game is governed; only then can it judge whether baseball is run well.

Most of the issues this book has addressed have solicited adherents to both sides largely because of a discernible lack of factual information about the commercial activities of baseball clubs, especially those facts pertaining to entry and financial performance. For example, without having financial information, some commentators have assumed that major-league baseball clubs are highly profitable. The financial analysis based on returns from all the clubs reveals that, in fact, most clubs lose money.

The controversies that have arisen out of imperfect information argue strongly that an appropriate solution to the governance issue may be found in promulgating to the public the rules governing entry and geographical exclusivity of franchises and in having the commissioner of baseball hold a periodic press conference on the state of professional baseball. Opening up the sport's aggregate financial performance and major transactions for all to see, and making such reports available to the public, would have obvious advantages over extending the complicated and technical provisions of the antitrust statutes and case law to an industry that in many vital respects does not fit the competitive market paradigm on which these statutes and judicial doctrines have been erected.

Notes

1. Roger Noll, ed., *Government and the Sports Business* (Washington: The Brookings Institution, 1974), p. 2.

2. George W. Stocking and Myron Watkins, *Cartels in Action* (New York: Twentieth Century Fund, 1946), p. 3.

3. See, for example, Walter C. Neale, "The Peculiar Economics of Professional Sports," *The Quarterly Journal of Economics* 78 (February 1964):1.

4. See table 5-1. The National League clubs, combined, earned a profit in 1974 and 1975, but suffered a loss in 1976 and 1977. The American League clubs, as a group, showed a reverse pattern, with losses in 1974 through 1976 and profits in 1977 and 1978.

5. There is some evidence that in the short run the addition of new entrants to a league may reduce an established club's total season attendance. The games the New York Yankees must give up with the Boston Red Sox to accommodate the Seattle Mariners would have yielded a higher attendance than the equal number of New York-Seattle games. (During their first two years of operation, Seattle and Toronto had the lowest road attendance in the American League.)

6. George Daly and William J. Moore, "Alternative Property Right Assignments and the Allocation of Resources: The Player Draft, the Reserve Clause, and Competition in Major League Baseball," forthcoming in *Economic Inquiry*, journal of the Western Economic Association (Spring 1981).

7. The territorial franchise, of course, pertains only to the league in which the club is a member, that is, the holder of the franchise cannot exercise it against clubs belonging to different leagues. (The specific limits are described later in this chapter.)

8. Developing the major-league schedule is surprisingly complex. Some years ago, a Harvard Business School doctoral student developed computer programs that could assist in the process, but he concluded the development of an efficient schedule was beyond the capabilities of any computer then available. Even with the computer's help, the annual schedule required several weeks of full-time effort. See William O. Cain, "Bayesian Discrete Optimizing as an Approach to a Scheduling Problem: Major League Baseball" (D.B.A. diss., Harvard Business School, 1972).

9. There is perhaps no area of endeavor in U.S. society having a more detailed and complete statistical bank of records than professional sports. This is so generally known that statisticians often use sports records to try out new techniques where either complete coverage or long time periods are critical.

10. In baseball, except for the Los Angeles Dodgers' park, all new ball parks constructed within the past fifty years have been publicly financed.

11. Stadia often involve a subsidy of one form or another, for example, reduced property taxes, reduced interest, or incomplete recovery of annual operating expenses. Unfortunately, not all public officials have always been forthright in revealing these subsidies to taxpayers or explaining the benefits such subsidies are intended to gain, which results in occasional outrage

stories in the press. On the other hand, many stadia involve little or no subsidy, and their leases are priced to recover full costs. Philadelphia, Pittsburgh, Cincinnati, and St. Louis appear to fit in this category, and no doubt there are others. Also, the Los Angeles Dodgers, the Chicago Cubs, the Chicago White Sox, and the Boston Red Sox own their stadia and pay property taxes on them.

12. U.S. Congress, House, Select Committee on Professional Sports, *Final Report* (Washington: USGPO, 1976), pt. 2, p. 383.

13. See, for example, Dan J. Gallagher, "An Economic Analysis of the Player Reservation System in the Professional Team Sports Industry in the United States" (Ph.D. diss., University of Maryland, August, 1976); Daly and Moore, "Alternative Property Right Assignments and the Allocation of Resources."

Appendix A:
Research Sources

In addition to a review of published materials concerning sports and especially baseball, the Cambridge Research Institute (CRI) collected information by means of surveys, samples from office records, review of players' contracts, review of unpublished documents, and personal and telephone interviews. The more important of these sources are listed.

Survey of Club Finances. A three-year history of detailed revenue and expense information was collected from the twenty-four clubs that existed prior to the 1977 expansion. The survey questionnaire was constructed along the lines of a Uniform Chart of Accounts that has been adopted by a number of clubs, so that most of the line items were figures that the clubs themselves used in the ordinary course of operations.

Clubs provided their data in confidence to Ernst & Whitney, then Ernst & Ernst, an independent accounting firm that has acted as outside auditors for four of the clubs and for the Office of the Commissioner and the Major Leagues Central Fund. Based on its baseball experience, Ernst & Ernst worked with the responding clubs to clarify definitions and attempted to ascertain that the data were in proper format. Ernst & Ernst made certain reclassifications and combinations to various expense categories as submitted by the clubs, but the survey results were not audited. CRI made spot checks to see whether clubs' responses were internally consistent and fell within "reasonable" ranges. The survey form is shown in figure A-1. [This survey has been repeated in 1978, 1979, and 1980. The tabulation for the 1979 season is shown in a later Appendix.]

Interviews with Club Owners and the Officials. Field interviews were held with eleven clubs owners and officials, to discuss many aspects of ownership and management of baseball clubs. During the course of this research, we met and held discussion with the managements of two minor-league clubs, the present and former executive directors of the Major League Baseball Player Relations Committee, the president of the National Association of Professional Baseball Leagues, and various other officials, staff members, coaches, and consultants associated with baseball and other sports.

Review of Player Contracts. CRI tabulated various information from player contracts for two seasons, made available by the league offices and the Player Relations Committee. These tabulations included salaries, the length of contracts, guarantees, bonuses, special types of compensation, length of major-league service and so forth.

Player Career Histories. The National Association of Professional Baseball Leagues maintains a career history for every professional player, showing the clubs he has played with, trades, and so on. From these records, we drew random samples and tabulated the training times in minor leagues, the "success rate" of minor leaguers in reaching the majors, and the "survival rate" of major-league players. Results are discussed in chapter 4.

Survey of Business Purchases. During the spring of 1978, the commissioner's office conducted a survey of the clubs, asking for their estimates of purchases of baseball tickets by business firms. Specifically of interest to CRI, the survey developed information concerning season-ticket purchases, average prices paid, and concessions purchases. (See "Statement of Bowie K. Kuhn, Commissioner of Baseball, before the House Ways and Means Committee, March 17, 1978.")

Study of Attendance and Market Potential. CRI conducted a statistical study (regression analysis) of baseball attendance in relation to city size, income, age, race, and other market-area characteristics. The results are discussed in chapter 4.

Commissioners' Office Records. From the commissioners' office files we drew on a host of items such as attendance records, ticket-price histories, Harris polls and other market studies, television contract information, and others.

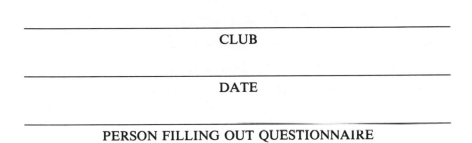

Figure A-1. Financial Information Questionnaire, Major-League Baseball, 1976 Season.

Table of Contents

Instructions for Completion of Questionnaire

Instructions for Completion of Questionnaire

Most of the items in this questionnaire are the same as those in the version which you submitted in 1972-1973. For convenience, we have placed specific instructions on the schedules to which they apply.

Some added information is being requested in this 1976 questionnaire to help prepare baseball's response to the congressional investigation of professional sports. These questions relate to such things as whether the club owns or leases its stadium, operates or contracts for its concessions, and so forth.

All data will be treated as strictly *confidential* and used only by Ernst & Ernst and by selected individuals at the Cambridge Research Institute for statistical analysis. Information which might reveal the identity of a particular club will not be disclosed to your league office, to the commissoner's office, to Congress, or to anyone else.

If you have any questions, please contact:

> Mr. John F. Wagner, Partner
> Ernst & Ernst
> 140 Broadway
> New York, New York   10005
> (212) 943-7800

General Instructions

1. Financial information should be for the fiscal year which includes the indicated playing season.
2. All amounts should be rounded to the nearest dollar.
3. All items in excess of $10,000 in any of the "Other" categories of the individual schedules should be listed and described separately.
4. All payroll taxes and insurance expenses should be included under general and administrative expenses, Schedule IX.

Schedule I: Baseball Operating Revenues
(Fiscal Year Ending _____)

A. *Game Receipts*
1. Regular-season home-game receipts, net of
admission taxes, league share, and visitors' shares $_____
2. Away-game receipts   _____
3. Receipts from exhibition games played during season
(include only games played after opening day)   _____
4. Total game receipts $_____

B. *Local Radio and Television*
(Note: Do not include league championship and World Series or Central Fund)
5. Does your club sell local radio and
television "rights" in a net package?   TV   ☐Yes   ☐No
                 Radio   ☐Yes   ☐No
6. If yes, net receipts for regular season: TV $_____
                        Radio
7. If no, revenue from sponsors for *regular season*
less station time charges, announcers' salaries,
production costs, line charges, and other
expenses   TV   _____
                        Radio   _____

Please indicate number of televised games:
     Home ____
     Away ____
Please indicate number of radio broadcast games:
     Home ____
     Away ____

C. *Park Concessions and Related Revenues* (Regular-season baseball games only)
8. Concessions income, net of expenses for regular
season $_____
Please indicate whether concessions are:
☐Club-operated   ☐Operated by an   ☐Operated by stadium   ☐Other
                  independent   owner or agent
                  contractor
9. Parking income, net of expenses, for regular season   _____
Please indicate whether parking is:
☐Club-operated   ☐Operated by stadium owner or   ☐Other
                               agent
10. Restaurant or stadium club income, net of expenses
for regular season   _____
Please indicate whether restaurant or stadium club is:
☐Club-operated   ☐Operated by an   ☐Operated by stadium   ☐Other
                  independent   owner or agent
                  contractor

11. Scoreboard, fence, and other advertising income, net
of expenses, for regular season _____
Please indicate whether advertising is:
☐Sold as "rights" in a   ☐Sold individually   ☐Other
  package deal   to each sponsor

12. Royalties and licensing fees, including
dividends from Major League Promotions Corp. _____

D. *League Championship and World Series*
13. Did your club play in:
League Championship   ☐Yes   ☐No
World Series   ☐Yes   ☐No
(Note: This information will not be tabulated in
        such a way as to identify individual clubs.)
If your club played in neither series, please skip to
line 22.

Clubs playing in League Championship or World Series

Please indicate whether the following figures are on:
☐"Accrual" basis   ☐"Cash" basis

14. Ticket sales, retained or distributed by league
office and commissioner's office $_____

15. Less: Unreimbursed expenses *directly* attributable
to league championship and World Series (for
example, hospitality room, ticket printing, travel
expenses, temporary construction, game operation
salaries, and ticket purchases for club use) (_____)

16. Net revenues from ticket sales
(line 14 less line 15) $_____

17. Local radio and television coverage of
league championship series—net _____

18. Concessions—net _____

19. Parking—net _____

20. Restaurant or Stadium Club—net _____

21. Advertising—net _____

22. League championship and World Series total
(lines 13 through 21) $_____

E. *Major Leagues Central Fund*
23. Receipts from Central Fund _____
Please indicate whether these receipts are on:
☐"Accrual" basis   ☐"Cash" basis

F. *Other Baseball-Related Net Operating Income*
24. Description (e.g., expansion payments)
_____   _____
_____

G. *Total Operating Revenues*
$_____

Schedule II: Spring Training Expenses
(Major-League Team Only)

1. Number of spring training days:

2. Number of spring training games:

3. Team reporting expenses $_____

4. Murphy and meal money   _____

5. Hotel and live-out allowance
   (players only)   _____

6. Home- and away-game expenses   _____

7. Office and club officials'
   expenses   _____

8. Other expenses (e.g., publicity,
   promotion, transportation to   _____
   opening season game)
   Describe if over $10,000:

   _____ $_____
   _____   _____
   _____   _____

9. Total expenses $_____

10. Less: Receipts from spring
    training games (include both
    home and away games and any
    games played en route to
    opening day)   (_____)

11. Total spring training
    expenses—net $_____

Note: Include only the expenses of the major-league team.
   Show minor-league expenses on Schedule IV.

Schedule III: Major-League Team Operating Expenses

1. Player salaries—Major-league
    service *only*
    a. Actual disbursements $_____
    b. Deferred compensation and
       other commitments chargeable
       to this season   _____

2. Other salaries, including manager,
    trainer, and coaching staff   _____

3. Transportation, hotels, meals,
    and related road-trip expenses   _____

4. Uniforms and playing equipment   _____

5. Baseballs   _____

6. Medical expenses, including team
    physician, supplies, hospital
    costs, etc.   _____

7. Laundry   _____

8. Players' moving allowances
    and expenses   _____

9. Other expenses—describe if over
    $10,000:   _____
    _____ $_____
    _____   _____
    _____   _____

10. Total team operating expenses $_____

Note: Include only the expenses of the major-league team.
       Show minor-league expenses on Schedule IV.

Schedule IV: Player Development Expenses

A. *Number of Minor-League Clubs*

   1. AAA   Owned _____   PDC _____

   2   AA   _____   _____

   3. A   _____   _____

   4. Rookie   _____   _____

   5. Number of days of minor-league spring training:

B. *Expenses*

   6. Salaries of farm director, player development director, assistants, and other administrative personnel $_____

   7. Salaries of pitching and batting coaches and instructors   _____

   8. Expenses of pitching and batting coaches and instructors   _____

       Player Development Contract (PDC) expenses[1]:

   9. Salaries (including major-league players on option)   _____

  10. Progress and incentive bonuses   _____

  11. Transportation home and assignments   _____

  12. Selection rights payment   _____

  13. Uniforms and equipment   _____

  14. Military allowance   _____

  15. Medical expenses   _____

  16. Makeup and rookie clubs   _____

  17. Other—describe if over $10,000.   _____

          _____ $_____

          _____   _____

          _____   _____

  18. Total PDC (lines 9 through 17) $_____

  19. Operating losses (income) of owned clubs[2]   _____

  20. National association fees   _____

  21. Winter instructional league   _____

  22. Spring training camps (exclusive of major-league team)—net   _____

  23. Other expenses—describe if over $10,000:   _____

          _____ $_____

          _____   _____

          _____   _____

  24. Total player development expenses $_____

[1]Include also the salaries, bonuses, transportation, etc., of *owned* clubs, if any.

[2]Include only those expenses (or revenues) that would not occur if player development contracts were in effect. The purpose of this procedure is to make comparable the costs of owned clubs and PDC clubs.

Schedule V: Team Replacement Costs and Expenses

A. *Scouting Expenses*
  1. Scouts' salaries, including "bird-dog" payments $_____
      Number of scouts: Full-time _____
                       Part-time _____
                       Bird-dogs _____
  2. Major-league scouting bureau   _____
  3. Travel expenses   _____
  4. Try-out camps   _____
  5. Amateur club expenses (exclusive of Central   _____
      Fund charges) and other
  6. Total scouting expenses $_____

B. *Player Acquisition Costs—Net of Dispositions*
  7. Amortization of initial roster cost: $_____
      Initial cost   _____
      Period to be amortized   _____ mos. or yrs.
      Year amortization commenced _____
      Note: If your club capitalizes players' contracts,
            please continue with lines 8 through 12.

            If your club is on the direct write-off method,
            please skip to line 13.

      Clubs That Capitalize Cost of Player Contracts
  8. Amortization of players' contracts $_____
  9. Unamortized cost of contracts for players released
      or retired during year   _____
 10. Draft and returns—net cost (income) on contracts
      acquired and disposed of during year   _____
 11. Net (gain) or loss on outright sale of contracts
      during year   _____
 12. College scholarship plan cost   _____
      Please skip to line 17

      Clubs on Direct Write-Off Method
 13. Bonuses to free agents $_____
 14. Purchase and sale of contracts—net   _____
 15. Expense (income) on players drafted and retired   _____
 16. College scholarship plan cost   _____
 17. Total player acquisition cost
      (Line 7 plus 8-12 or 13-16) $_____
 18. Total team replacement costs $_____

Schedule VI: Stadium Operation Expenses

1. Does your club own or rent its
   stadium?
   ☐ Own   ☐ Rent

2. Stadium rent (if not owned).
   Please indicate additional
   services that are included as
   a part of rental. $_____
       ☐ Security
       ☐ Groundskeeping
       ☐ Heat, light, power
       ☐ Maintenance
       ☐ Property taxes
       ☐ Other—describe:

3. Salaries, for baseball games
   (including ushers, grounds crews,
   cleaning personnel, and so forth)   _____

4. Wages of ticket sellers for
   "day of game only"   _____

5. Security service—outside gate   _____

6. Light, heat, and power   _____

7. Maintenance and repairs   _____

8. Property taxes   _____

9. Playing field maintenance—
   sod, landscaping, etc.   _____

10. Depreciation and amortization of
    stadium and/or its equipment   _____

11. Other expenses—describe if
    over $10,000:   _____
        _____ $_____
        _____   _____
        _____   _____

12. Total stadium operation
    expenses $_____

Note: Salaries and other direct expenses for nonbaseball events should be netted against nonbaseball revenue and recorded on Schedule X. Salaries and expenses directly attributable to league championship and World Series should be netted against league championship and World Series revenues and recorded on Schedule I, section D.

Schedule VII: Ticket Department Expenses

1. Salaries of ticket department $_____
    (excluding "day of game only"
    personnel which should be
    recorded on Schedule VI)

2. Rent and other expenses of remote   _____
    locations

3. Ticket printing and schedules   _____

4. Postage, commissions, armored-   _____
    car services, and other ticket-
    related expenses—describe
    if over $10,000:

    _____ $_____

    _____   _____

    _____   _____

5. Total ticket department
    expenses $_____

Note: Expenses of regular baseball season only. Ticket department expenses directly attributable to league championship series and World Series should be netted against league championship series and World Series revenues and recorded on Schedule I, section D.

Schedule VIII: Publicity and Promotion Expenses

1. Salaries (publicity and promotion
    directors, assistants, clerical) $_____

2. Travel and reimbursed expenses   _____

3. Press room expenses (salaries and
    food, etc., but not press box
    attendants)   _____

4. Special events (opening day,
    Oldtimers, giveaways, other game
    promotions)   _____

5. Dinners and testimonials, newspaper
    advertising, and other publicity
    and promotion expenses—describe
    if over $10,000:   _____

    _____ $_____
    _____   _____
    _____   _____

6. Total publicity and promotion
    expenses $_____

Note: Salaries and expenses directly attributable to league championship series and World Series should be netted against league championship series and World Series revenues and recorded on Schedule I, section D.

Schedule IX: General and Administrative Expenses

1. Salaries—officers, executive, $_____
    clerical

2. Travel and entertainment   _____

3. Office rent, light, heat   _____

4. Telephone   _____

5. Legal   _____

6. Audit   _____

7. Payroll taxes (for all personnel,   _____
    including players, scouts, coaches,
    stadium personnel, and so forth)

8. Business taxes other than payroll,   _____
    income, real estate

9. Nonplayer employee benefits   _____
    (include health, life and dis-
    ability insurance, workmen's
    compensation, profit-sharing
    and pension plans)

10. Insurance, including liability,   _____
    team travel and disaster, fire,
    and other

11. Postage (exclusive of ticket   _____
    department)

12. Stationery, printing, and   _____
    office supplies

13. Depreciation and amortization   _____
    other than pertaining to stadium
    and players' contracts

14. Umpire development program   _____
    (American League only)

15. Other—describe if over $10,000:   _____
    _____ $_____
    _____   _____
    _____   _____

16. Total general and
    administrative expenses $_____

Note: Salaries and expenses directly attributable to league championship series and World Series should be netted against league championship series and World Series revenues and recorded on Schedule I, section D.

Schedule X: Summary of Operating Income and Expenses

Baseball Operations

1. Operating revenues—Schedule I $_____
   Operating expenses:
2. Spring training—Schedule II   _____
3. Team operating—Schedule III   _____
4. Player development—Schedule IV   _____
5. Team replacement—Schedule V   _____
6. Stadium operation—Schedule VI   _____
7. Ticket department—Schedule VII   _____
8. Publicity and promotion—Schedule VIII   _____
9. General and administrative—Schedule IX   _____
10. Total expenses $_____
11. Income (loss) from baseball operations $_____
12. Over the past 10 years (1967 through 1976) please indicate:
    a. Number of years in which net income from
        baseball operations (line 12) was a profit   ____
    b. Number of years in which net income from
        baseball operations (line 12) was a loss   ____

Other Income (Expense)

13. Stadium rentals from nonbaseball $_____
    activities—net of expenses
14. Investment income (expense)—net   _____
15. Miscellaneous income (expense)—net   _____
    Describe if over $10,000:
        _____ $_____
        _____   _____
        _____   _____
16. Total other income (expense) $_____
17. Total income (loss) before
    income taxes $_____

Appendix B:
Player Development
Contract

THIS AGREEMENT, made this_____day of_____19_____ by and between

_____ hereinafter referred to as Selector,

and_____ hereinafter referred to as Selectee;

WITNESSETH:

Selectee operates a professional baseball club in_____League (a Class_____League) and desires the assistance of Selector in assembling a team of professional baseball players qualified to play in its league.

Selector conducts a training program designed to develop players for service with Selector, and desires to use Selectee's facilities to develop the playing skills of certain players.

To accomplish their respective objectives and to comply with the Professional Baseball Rules, Selector and Selectee recognize that it is necessary and in their mutual interest:

(a) For Selectee to own and assume the primary responsibility for the contracts of all players on its roster;

(b) For Selector to reimburse Selectee for certain expenses in respect to players provided for Selectee by Selector; and

(c) For Selector to be able, as hereinafter provided, to exercise its judgment respecting the acquisition and disposition of player contracts provided for Selectee by Selector and the training and advancement of the players involved.

NOW, THEREFORE, in consideration of the premises and of the exchange of undertakings herein, the parties agree as follows:

1. Provision for Selectee's Roster.

(a) Selector shall provide, and maintain throughout the season, a roster of skilled players. The minimum number of players to be provided by Selector shall be:

Class A   — 18
Class AA   — 19
Class AAA — 21

unless Selectee desires to provide one or more players, in which case responsibility for maintaining the roster shall be divided as follows:

Selector_____   Selectee_____

If Selectee is Class AAA, the limit of 21 players shall apply from the opening date to 20 days before the close of the season, at which time the limit shall become 24 active players, but any additions made in that period must consist of players whose contracts were assigned outright by, or recalled from optional assignment from, a club of Class AA or lower. The Selectee's season shall open not later than 5 days after commencement of the Major League season and shall close on or before Labor Day.

(b) The undertakings of the parties under paragraph 1(a) hereof may be changed by mutual agreement, written notice of which shall be given the Commissioner, the President of the National Association and the President of Selector's League.

2. Selectable and Non—Selectable Players. Any and all players on the roster of Selectee, including players on optional assignment, and any players on the Suspended, Disabled, Temporarily Inactive, Voluntarily Retired, Restricted, Disqualified, Ineligible and Military Lists of Selectee, shall be known as Selectable Players and as such subject to paragraph 3 hereof, except the following Non—Selectable Players:

Class I—Players provided by Selectee under paragraph 1. The Commissioner and the President of the National Association shall be notified promptly of the identity of such players by a written notice signed by officers of Selector and Selectee.

Class II—Players acquired under optional assignment from clubs other than Selector or an affiliate of Selector.

Class III—Players selectable by any other Selector under a Player Development Contract.

3. Contracts of Selectable Players.

(a) Selectee agrees to execute contracts of Selectable Players, a team manager and coaches with persons and at terms satisfactory to the Selector.

(b) Selector shall have the right to select the contracts of any or all Selectable Players on or before December 15, 19

(c) Selector shall have (1) the right at any time to direct the release, optional assignment and optional recall of the contracts of Selectable Players by Selectee, subject to the provisions of paragraph 8, and (2) the right to direct the outright assignment of the contracts of Selectable Players by Selectee except during the period beginning 15 days prior to the opening of Selectee's season and ending with the close of Selectee's season and any play-off or official post-season series in which Selectee participates, and (3) the right at any time to direct the assignment of contracts of Selectable Players to the Selector or to an affiliate of the Selector of higher classification than the Selectee provided that no such assignment shall be in conflict with the second paragraph of Professional Baseball Rule 11(b).

4. Manager of Selectee. Selector shall name the team manager, unless Selectee is Class AAA, in which case Selectee may name the manager, subject to approval of Selector, which shall not be unreasonably withheld.

5. Payments by Selector. Selector shall pay or provide for the following:

(a) The consideration, or fee, for the acquisition of the contract of a Selectable Player; and the Uniform Player Contract filing fee for a Selectable Player.

(b) Any bonus payment required under the contract of a Selectable Player signed as a free agent;

(c) All spring training expenses for Selectee's team at a site and for a period to be designated by Selector, including the travel expenses of players reporting to the training camp, the travel expense from the training camp to the city where the team is scheduled to open the season, and the hotel and meal allowances of the team in such city from date of arrival through the day preceding the official opening of the season.

(d) All travel expenses of any Selectable Player to his home by air coach or other transportation with equivalent fare if the player's contract, with the Selector's approval, requires such payment;

(e) All travel expenses of Selectable Players arising from assignment of their contracts during the regular season and payable by Selectee under the Professional Baseball Rules;

(f) If Selectee is Class AA or A, Selector shall furnish one set of uniforms in good condition; or, at Selectee's option, Selector shall pay up to a maximum of Fifteen Hundred Dollars ($1,500.00) to be designated for the purchase of uniforms approved by Selector, and payable upon presentation of a bona fide statement from the company supplying the uniforms. "Set" shall consist of not less than 26 uniforms plus four extra pants. Each uniform would include shirt, pants, belt, and outer socks.

135

(g) If Selectee is Class AAA, Selector shall pay all of its travel, hotel and miscellaneous expense in connection with an exhibition game it plays in Selectee's city, all of the revenue from such game to be the property of Selectee; provided, however, that if such exhibition game is not possible or practicable in the judgment of Selector, Selector shall pay Selectee the sum of $5,000, which payment shall be transmitted to the Class AAA club not later than October 1 of the particular year. If an exhibition game which has been scheduled in accordance with this provision cannot be played because of rain or other cause beyond the control of Selectee, Selector shall pay Selectee the sum of $5,000; provided, however, that if Selector's team has traveled to Selectee's city in anticipation of the playing of such game, Selector may deduct the actual cost of its travel from the payment due Selectee.

(h) **For the current season only,** as a special consideration for the selection rights granted under this contract, Selector shall pay Selectee the amount indicated below:

> If Selectee is Class AAA $5,000
> If Selectee is Class AA $3,000
> If Selectee is Class A $1,500

Payment under this provision shall be contingent upon Selectee completing the current season, during which it must have complied with its obligation under Section 7 of this contract to provide transportation, meal money, playing conditions and equipment commensurate with the classification of its league and satisfactory to the Selector. Selectee shall also furnish Selector with financial operating statements. Payment shall be made not later than November 1, of the current season, by check payable to and transmitted through the National Association.

6.   **Reimbursement of Selectee.**

(a) Selector shall reimburse Selectee semi-monthly for:
(1) All Salary paid Selectable Players on the Active List of the Selectee in excess of the following amounts:
> Class A   -   Selector reimburses all salary of all Selectable Players.
> Class AA   - $150 per player per month ($5 per day) on nineteen (19) Selectable Players, plus the entire salary of all Selectable Players in excess of nineteen (19).
> Class AAA   - $450 per player per month ($15 per day) on twenty (20) Selectable Players, plus the entire salary of all Selectable Players in excess of twenty (20).

(2) Selectee's entire salary obligation to any Selectable Players in addition to the number covered by Paragraph 1 who are carried on Selectee's active list before cutdown date or during the final 20 days of the season;

(3) Selectee's entire salary obligations to Selectable Players on any inactive list;

(4) Selectee's entire salary obligations to Selectable Players whose contracts have been assigned, optionally or outright, by Selectee with approval of Selector;

(5) Selectee's entire salary obligation to the team manager if Selectee is Class AA or A, or if Selectee is Class AAA and Selector names the manager. If Selectee is Class AAA and names the manager, Selector shall reimburse Selectee for salary up to $7,500 per season;

(6) Selectee's entire salary obligation to any coach employed at the request of Selector; and

(7) Payroll taxes and workmen's compensation premiums based upon the amount of such reimbursements. Upon receipt of written proof of amount of deposit required by the insurance carried before workmen's compensation insurance shall become effective, Selector agrees to advance the deposit required less any amount applicable to coverage not subject to reimbursement by Selector. Selectee shall furnish Selector with copy of Certificate of Insurance Coverage. Selector shall be entitled to pro-rate the amount of its advance deposit over the course of the playing season and take proper credit when reimbursing Selectee under provisions of this Section 6(a).

(8) If Selectee is Class AAA and participates in a league play-off series, Selector's obligation to reimburse salary in excess of $450 per month per Selectable Player shall be extended for the duration of such intra-league play-off series.

(9) In addition to the salary required to be reimbursed under paragraph (2) of this section 6(a), Selector shall reimburse Selectee for all other costs incident to the carrying of Selectable players, before cutdown date or during the final 20 days of the season, in excess of the number of such players Selector has agreed to furnish Selectee. Selectee shall be responsible for all other costs incident to the field manager, even though the field manager is carried as a player-manager.

(10) To facilitate the reimbursement provided for in this Section 6(a), Selector shall notify Selectee at least two weeks in advance of the opening of the season which one of the following arrangements shall be in effect for that season:
(A) Selector shall itself handle all payrolls included in this section 6(a) and Selectee agrees to reimburse Selector within seven (7) days of receipt of billing for its share of salaries, payroll taxes and workmen's compensation premiums based upon its obligations under this contract.

(B) Selector shall establish a payroll account in Selectee's city and shall maintain a sufficient balance in such account to cover the amount of its obligations for salary, payroll taxes and workmen's compensation premiums for each payroll period.

(C) Selector shall forward to Selectee in time to arrive at Selectee's mailing address by the 13th and 28th of each month during the season the amount necessary to cover its obligations for salary, payroll taxes and workmen's compensation premiums for the payroll period. If the 15th or 30th falls on a Sunday or holiday, the payments shall arrive not later than the 12th or 27th respectively. Selectee must furnish payroll information by the 8th and 23rd of each month.

Selectee shall submit to Selector its statement of salary payments and other miscellaneous expenses subject to reimbursement by the 15th and 30th of each month and shall refund within seven (7) days thereafter any balance remaining from payment received. Selector shall reimburse Selectee within seven (7) days of receipt of statement for any balance not covered by earlier payment.

(11) Selector shall reimburse Selectees within seven (7) days of receipt of statement for the following expense items:

(A) Meal Allowances as defined in Section 7(d) and entire allowances of players in excess of twenty (20) if Class AAA, nineteen (19) if Class AA, or eighteen (18) if Class A.

(B) Hotel Expenses on road of players in excess of twenty (20) if Class AAA, nineteen (19) if Class AA, or eighteen (18) if Class A.

(C) Reporting and transportation home, including miscellaneous expenses of Selectable Players, field manager and coach as provided in their Uniform Player Contract; transportation home of trainer; transportation for players fulfilling military reserve or national guard requirements if approved by Selector; as well as any other transportation furnished by Selectee at direction and with approval of Selector.

(D) Commercial fare air transportation charges while traveling in league for players in excess of twenty (20) if Class AAA, nineteen (19) if Class AA, or eighteen (18) if Class A.

6. (a)   (11) continued

(E) All costs during the playing season incident to any coach employed at the request of Selector.

(F) All obligations to be paid by Selector to Selectee under this rule must be submitted by Selectee to Selector no later than December 31, immediately following the conclusion of the season for which the obligations are to be paid in order for Selector to be required to pay those obligations. Likewise, all obligations to be paid by Selectee to Selector under this rule must be submitted by Selector to Selectee no later than December 31, immediately following the conclusion of the season for which the obligations are to be paid in order for Selectee to be required to pay those obligations.

(b) Selector shall not be obligated to reimburse Selectee for any salary paid to Non—Selectable Players.

7. Selectee's Obligations.

(a) Selectee shall reimburse Selector for spring training expense of Non—Selectable Players. Payment shall be made promptly upon presentation of bill by Selector.

(b) Selectee shall not acquire Class I Non—Selectable Players in addition to the number specified in paragraph 1, without consent of Selector.

(c) Selectee shall consult with Selector on the opening day and duration of the season's schedule and on any proposed change in its league circuit, and shall be governed by Selector on any legislation pertaining to classification of players.

(d) Selectee shall pay its players meal money as follows for each day the club is scheduled to play away from home: If Selectee is Class AAA, the sum of Twelve Dollars ($12.00), of which Four Dollars and Fifty Cents ($4.50) shall be reimbursed by Selector; if Class AA, the sum of Nine Dollars and Fifty Cents ($9.50), of which Five dollars and Fifty Cents ($5.50) shall be reimbursed by Selector; if Class A, the sum of Eight Dollars and Fifty Cents ($8.50), of which Five Dollars and Fifty Cents ($5.50), shall be reimbursed by Selector. However, if it is possible for the club to commute back and forth to the city in which it is scheduled to play, then the club may pay the players one half of the normal allowance; if Class AAA, Selector shall reimburse Selectee Two Dollars and Twenty-five Cents ($2.25) per day; if Class AA or Class A, Selector shall reimburse Selectee Two Dollars and Seventy-five Cents ($2.75) per day.

(e) The condition of the vehicle or vehicles used to transport the team shall be subject to approval by Selector, provided that decision as to its or their acceptability shall be made prior to opening of spring training.

(f) Selectee agrees to furnish a reasonable amount of baseballs for club workouts and batting practice; to keep its uniforms in good repair and to have them cleaned when needed; and to make sure the players have an adequate supply of bats of their choosing on hand at all times during the season.

8. Releases and Assignments.

(a) Selector shall have the right to direct the release of Selectable Players, subject to the following:

(1) No Selectable Player shall be released during the season without Selectee's consent. If such release is proposed by Selector, Selectee may elect to retain the player as a Class I Non—Selectable Player. Any bonus payments and any salary which shall become due to such player on and after the date of such election by Selectee shall be the responsibility of Selectee. Written notice of the change in such player's status, jointly signed by the Selector and Selectee, shall immediately be given to the Commissioner and the President of the National Association.

(b) Selector shall have the right to direct the release of the team manager and any coach, except a manager in Class AAA and any coach appointed by Selectee.

(c) If the contract of a Selectable Player is assigned, the consideration therefor, if any, shall be remitted to Selector by the National Association.

(d) Selectee shall not assign the contract of any Class I Non—Selectable Player until after Selector has been given 72 hours from the time of dispatch of telegraphic notice of Selectee's intention to assign such contract, during which period Selector shall have the right to purchase such contract for the consideration set forth below:

Class A   — $ 5,000 plus Selectee's Investment;
Class AA   — $10,000 plus Selectee's Investment;
Class AAA — $20,000 plus Selectee's Investment.

"Selectee's Investment" shall be limited to:

(1) The consideration paid by Selectee for acquisition of the contract; or

(2) The amount of bonus, if any, paid to the player if signed by Selectee as a free agent.

If Selectee has not been notified, at the expiration of 72 hours from time of dispatch of its notice, that Selector desires to purchase the contract, Selectee may assign the contract at its discretion during the period ending ten days after the time of dispatch of its notice.

(e) If, during the championship season, the Selectee does not desire to retain a Selectable Player, it shall give the Selector telegraphic notice of that fact. Within five days after date of such notice (exclusive of Saturday and Sunday), the Selector may (i) exercise its right to select the player's contract, or (ii) authorize the Selectee to release the player unconditionally, or (iii) designate a club to which the contract is to be assigned by the Selectee. If the Selector fails to act, the Selectee may release the player unconditionally but may not re-sign him during the current season without Selector's consent. The Selector shall have the option itself to fill the vacancy created by disposition of the contract or to authorize the Selectee to fill it with a Non—Selectable Player. The Selectee's right to give notice under this subparagraph (e) shall be limited during any season to an aggregate of three players if Selectee is Class AAA, two players if Selectee is Class AA, and one player if Selectee if Class A.

(f) Selector shall have the right to select players for Selectee's Negotiation List under Professional Baseball rule 4, and such players, if signed, shall be Selectable Players.

(g) Selector shall have the right to receive, prepare and file Selectee's selection list with the Commissioner's office and Selectee's reserve list with the President of the National Association, which lists when filed shall include the contracts of Class I Non—Selectable players specified in Section 1.(a).

9. Selection of Class I Non—Selectable Players. Selector shall have the right to select the contracts of any Class I Non—Selectable Players during the period beginning with the close of Selectee's championship season and ending October 1, for the consideration set forth in paragraph 8(d).

10. Extent of Selector's Obligations. Except as specified in this Agreement, Selector does not assume and shall not have, by implication or otherwise, any obligation or responsibility to the Selectee or with respect to the operation of the Selectee's business or with respect to its players or player contracts.

11. Professional Baseball Rules.

(a) All rights and liabilities of Selector and Selectee set forth in Professional Baseball Rule 10(d) are hereby made part of this contract; and

(b) No action shall be taken under this contract which conflicts with the Professional Baseball Agreement or Rules.

12. Notices. All notices, directions, requests, consents and other communications hereunder shall be given by registered or certified mail or by telegram.

13. Filing. Executed copies of this Agreement shall be filed with the Commissioner, the President of the National Association and the Presidents of Selector's and Selectee's Leagues.

14. Effective Date. This contract shall be effective from the date hereof until **December 15, 19_____**, and shall continue in effect from year to year thereafter unless written notice of termination is given by either party to the other party and to the Commissioner and the President of the National Association on or before November 1 of the year of termination.

IN WITNESS WHEREOF, the parties have executed this Agreement by their respective officers thereunto duly authorized as of the date above written.

Selector Club _____

By _____

Selectee Club _____

By _____

Other Regulations

(a) The amounts set forth in the Player Development Contract for specific items shall not be changed, but the Selector, in its discretion, may make payments to the Selectee for items not included in the standard contract.

(b) In the event either party terminates the Player Development Contract on or before November 1, the Selectee shall be entitled to sign free agents and acquire player contracts during the period October 20 through December 15 in an amount equal to its under control limit; provided, however, that any players on the Selectee's roster on October 20, subject to possible selection by the Selector, shall not be counted against the Selectee's under control limit during the period October 20 through December 15; and provided further, that the Selectee shall bring its roster within its under control limit by midnight December 15.

(c) In the event the Player Development Contract is terminated on or before November 1, the Selector shall have the right to select only those contracts held by the Selectee on October 20. However, Selector shall have the right to select from Selectee the contracts of any players acquired by Selectee through the player draft at the annual meetings. The consideration for such a selection shall be One Hundred Dollars ($100.00) plus the consideration paid by Selectee for acquisition of the player's contract. Other contracts acquired by the Selectee after that date shall not be subject to selection under the Player Development Contract.

Effect of Disbandment.

(a) Should a selectee for any reason decide to disband or otherwise cease operations, it shall give the Selector not less than five (5) days' written or telegraphic notice of such intention prior to the contemplated date of disbandment during which period said Selector shall have the right to select the contracts of Selectable Players, or to direct assignments thereof, without liability for any payments beyond those already due or paid prior to date of such notice.

(b) In the event the Selectee should cease operations prior to the final date set forth in the Player Development Contract for selection of player contracts, the following shall apply:

(1) The Selector's right to select player contracts or to direct the assignment thereof shall not be impaired, notwithstanding anything to the contrary in Sections 10.07 and 30.13, National Association Agreement.

(2) For purposes of Professional Baseball Rule 11 (L), the Commissioner or the President of the National Association, as the case may be, may consider the selection of any player contract that is subsequently reassigned within fifteen (15) days, as equivalent to a direct assignment by the Selectee to the ultimate assignee, and the player's optional record shall be marked accordingly.

(3) The Commissioner or the President of the National Association, as the case may be, may approve the selection of a player's contract which normally would not be approvable under Professional Baseball Rule 11 (L), provided the contract is subsequently reassigned, within fifteen (15) days, to an affiliate club of the same or lower classification than that of the Selectee, or to an unaffiliated club of any classification.

Effect of Draft.   In any case where a player contract which was subject to selection under a Player Development Contract has been drafted, the Selector under the Player Development Contract shall be entitled to the consideration paid for the draft and the President of the National Association shall transmit such payment to the Selector.

Printed in U.S.A. — Revised as of 9-79

Appendix C:
Sources for Figure 4-3

**Principal Revenues and Expenses
in the Baseball Industry**

All figures are three-year averages for 1975-1977.

1. Rental of stadiums to nonbaseball users: Clubs' financial survey, Schedule X.
2. Fees charged to scoreboard and fence advertisers, etc.: Clubs' financial survey, Schedule I.
3. Gate receipts from spring training games: Clubs' financial survey, Schedule II.
4. Investments and miscellaneous revenue: Clubs' financial survey, Schedule X.
5. Amusement and admissions taxes calculated by scaling up the 1962 figure according to the three-year average attendance for 1975-1977. The 1962 figure is taken from "Baseball in the Community" (Xeroxed excerpt received from commissioner's office).
6. Interest expense: Clubs' financial survey, Schedule X.
7. Spring training expense: Clubs' financial survey, Schedule II.
8. Publicity and promotion expense: Clubs' financial survey, Schedule VIII.
9. General and administrative expense: Clubs' financial survey, Schedule IX.
10. Other stadium operation expense: Clubs' financial survey, Schedule VI.
11. Revenue to concessionaires from attendance at regular-season games: calculated by multiplying major-league clubs' net income from concessions, parking, and restaurant or stadium clubs as found in clubs' financial survey, Schedule I, by 2.5, and approximate ratio provided to CRI by several clubs. This ratio is conservative, since many clubs receive little or none of the concessions at their parks.
12. Gate receipts from regular-season games: Clubs' financial survey, Schedule I, plus admission taxes (see item 5) plus leagues' share of gate receipts (see item 49).
13. Stadium operation expenses: Clubs' financial survey, Schedule VI.
14. Rentals paid to public stadium authorities: Clubs' financial survey, Schedule VI.
15. Major-league clubs' net income from concessionaires (concessions, parking, and restaurant or stadium clubs): Clubs' financial survey, Schedule I.

16. Player development expenses: Clubs' financial survey, Schedule IV.
17. Farm-system expenses other than contract payments and operating losses: Clubs' financial survey, Schedule IV.
18. Winter and spring training (other than major league): Clubs' financial survey, Schedule IV.
19. Gate receipts from minor-league games: Estimated as approximately $1.00 per fan, a rule of thumb mentioned by several minor-league contacts.
20. Farm-system contract payments and operating losses: Clubs' financial survey, Schedule IV.
21. Other expenses of minor-league clubs: Calculated by subtracting itemized expenses from minor-league clubs' total revenues (assumes minor-league clubs break even, which may not be the case).
22. Salaries of minor-league players: Clubs' financial survey, Schedule IV, "working agreement expenses."
23. Team replacement expenses: Clubs' financial survey, Schedule V.
24. Bonuses to minor-league players: Clubs' financial survey, Schedule V, "amortization of player contracts" plus "bonuses to free agents" plus college scholarship plans.
25. Depreciation and capital losses (or gains) (team replacement expenses other than bonuses to minor-league players and scouting expenses): Clubs' financial survey, Schedule V.
26. Scouts and scouting bureau: Clubs' financial survey, Schedule V, "total scouting expenses."
26a. Advertising revenue to local TV and radio stations: No specific attempt was made to determine these revenues. One author, Roger Noll, has estimated these amounts as 2 to 2½ times the amount paid to clubs.
27. Revenue to major-league clubs from local TV and radio stations: Clubs' financial survey, Schedule I.
28. Team operation expenses: Clubs' financial survey, Schedule III.
29. Travel and additional team expenses other than players' salaries: Clubs' financial survey, Schedule III.
30. Major-league players' salaries: Clubs' financial survey, Schedule III, "actual disbursements" plus "deferred compensation."
31. Revenue from concessionaires at league championship and World Series games: clubs' financial survey, Schedule I.
32. Revenue to major-league clubs from Major Leagues Promotions Corporation (estimate provided by the commissioner's office).
33. Revenue to major-league clubs from the Major Leagues Central Fund: Audited financial statements of the Major Leagues Central Fund, Statement of Transactions, "deductions."
34. Revenue to major-league clubs from the League Championship and World Series Fund: Clubs' financial survey, Schedule I.
35. Clubs' operating gain or loss: Clubs' financial survey, Schedule I.
36. Income to Players from the League Championship and World Series

Fund: Clubs' financial survey, Schedule I, portion of proceeds from ticket sales distributed to players.

37. Income to Players' Benefit Trust from the Major Leagues Central Fund: Audited financial statements of the Major Leagues Central Fund, Statement of Transactions.

38. Revenue to Major Leagues Central Fund from national TV and radio networks: Audited financial statements of the Major Leagues Central Fund, Statement of Transactions.

39. Gate receipts from all-star game: Audited financial statements of the Major Leagues Central Fund, Statement of Transactions.

40. Interest and miscellaneous income: Audited financial statements of the Major Leagues Central Fund, Statement of Transactions.

41. Expenditures of Major Leagues Central Fund from national TV and radio networks, all-star game gate receipts, and interest and miscellaneous income: Audited financial statement of the Major Leagues Central Fund, Statement of Transactions.

42. Revenue to concessionaires from attendance at league championship and World Series games: Ernst & Ernst tabulation reported with clubs' financial survey, Schedule I, "concessions" figure multiplied by 2.5, the share estimate provided to CRI by the clubs.

43. Gate receipts from league championship and World Series games: Ernst & Ernst tabulation reported with clubs' financial survey, Schedule I, sum of amounts distributed to players, office of the commissioner, leagues, and clubs.

44. League Championship and World Series Fund monies distributable to players, office of the commissioner, leagues, and clubs (gate receipts less expenses): Ernst & Ernst tabulation.

45. Portion of the League Championship and World Series Fund distributed to the office of the commissioner: Ernst & Ernst tabulation, reported with clubs' financial survey, Schedule I.

46. Portion of the Major Leagues Central Fund distributed to the office of the commissioner: Audited financial statement of the Major Leagues Central Fund, Statement of Transactions.

47. Portion of the Major Leagues Central Fund distributed to the Player Relations Committee: Audited financial statement of the Major Leagues Central Fund, Statement of Transactions.

48. Portion of the League Championship and World Series Fund distributed to the league offices: Ernst & Ernst tabulation reported with clubs' financial survey, Schedule I.

49. Leagues' share of gate receipts: Annual reports of the leagues (American League Statement of Revenues and Expenses, National League Report on Operations).

50. Umpire and umpire development expenses: Annual reports of the leagues: American League Annual Report, umpire and games expenses, under "general expenses, umpire development." National League

Annual Report, comparative expenses, within the "game expense" category, "umpire salaries," "umpire expense," "umpire purchase," and "umpire observation—consultation" are included. Within the "pensions" category, "umpires' retirement" and "retired umpires, employees" are included.

51. Contributions from the Major Leagues Central Fund to little leagues, etc.: Audited financial statement of the Major Leagues Central Fund, Statement of Transactions, sum of "contributions."

52. Miscellaneous joint expenses (includes baseball promotion expenses, professional fees, Hall of Fame member grants, all-star game expenses, etc.): Audited financial statement of the Major Leagues Central Fund, Statement of Transactions.

Additional Detail for Selected Funds Flows on Figure 4-3

Item 9: General and Administrative Expenses

Personnel:	$000	%
Salaries	6,958	26.7
Payroll taxes, workmen's compensation (note 1), and nonplayer benefits	6,713	24.8
Travel and entertainment	1,400	5.4
Outside professional service (note 2)	2,085	8.0
Insurance	2,957	11.4
Depreciation and amortization	1,112	4.3
Office operations (note 3)	2,788	10.7
Taxes, bad debts (note 4) other—Notes	2,025	7.8
Total	26,039	100.0

Note 1: Not shown separately for seasons prior to 1977.

Note 2: Includes "audit", "legal" and in 1977 other "professional services" not previously shown separately.

Note 3: Includes "telephone," "postage," "stationary," "office rent," "light, heat" and in 1977 "dues and subscriptions," "computer services" "office rental and repairs," and "office cleaning" not previously shown separately.

Note 4: Not shown separately for seasons prior to 1977.

Note 5: Prior to 1977 category includes umpire development: 1975: $31,000; 1976: $41,500 (because of rounding amounts do not add to total).

Item 13: Combined Stadium Operation Expenses

	$000	%
Rent	7,160	22.3
Salaries including ushers ground crews, cleaning personnel, ticket sellers on game day	13,577	42.2
Maintenance and repairs	4,759	14.8
Depreciation and amortization	2,903	9.0
Property taxes	1,723	5.4
Other (note 1)	2,042	6.3
Total	32,164	100.0

Note 1: Includes "security services," "other," and in 1977 "uniforms and laundry," "medical service," "music-related expenses," and "rubbish removal," not shown separately in previous years.

Item 28: Major League Team Operating Expenses

	$000	%
Salaries, players actual and deferred	39,700	70.5
Salaries (not players')— managers, coaches, etc.	4,583	8.1
Travel, including transportation baggage, hotels, meals, and related expenses	8,713	15.5
Uniforms and playing equipment	645	1.1
Baseballs and bats	671	1.2
Medical expenses, including team physician, supplies, hospital costs, etc.	469	.8
Players' moving allowance and expenses	202	.4
Laundry and clubhouse supplies	295	.5
Other (note 1)	1,029	1.8
Total	56,306	100.0

Note 1: Includes workmen's compensation and umpire development (because of rounding, amounts do not add to total).

Appendix D:
Summary of Financial
Survey Report

Certain Financial Data (Unaudited): Major-League Baseball, 1977, 1976, 1975, and 1974 Seasons

CONTENTS

Ernst & Ernst

Citicorp Center • 153 East 53rd Street • New York, New York 10022 • Phone 212/752-8100

July 31, 1978

Baseball - Office of the Commissioner
15 West 51st Street
New York, N. Y.

Gentlemen:

At your request, we have corresponded with each of the major league
baseball clubs, requesting that certain financial data for the 1977
season be supplied to us. The accompanying summary and schedules reflect
a summarization of such data, along with similar data for the 1976, 1975,
and 1974 seasons, and as requested, also include the income and expenses
of the Major Leagues Central Fund for each of the years ended October 31,
1977, 1976, 1975 and 1974. Certain reclassifications and combinations
have been made to various expense categories as submitted by the
individual clubs; in addition, the summary and schedules for 1977 and
1976 do not include any amounts for money received or accrued in
connection with the American League expansion draft which took place
subsequent to the end of the 1976 season.

Inasmuch as we have not made an examination of such summary, schedules
or data, other than the income and expenses of the Major Leagues Central
Fund, we are unable to and do not express any opinion on them.

Very truly yours,

Ernst + Ernst

E&E

COMBINED SUMMARY OF OPERATIONS
(BEFORE INCOME TAXES) (UNAUDITED)

MAJOR LEAGUE BASEBALL

SCHEDULE 1

	Schedule	1977	%	1976	%	1975	%	1974	%
OPERATING REVENUES, including receipts of Major Leagues Central Fund	Schedule II	$230,975,344		$180,940,901		$160,769,926		$152,110,530	
OPERATING EXPENSES									
Spring training	Schedule III	2,704,278	1.2	2,148,134	1.2	2,552,792	1.5	2,592,366	1.6
Team	Schedule IV	82,743,446	35.4	60,563,162	32.6	52,317,866	31.8	47,954,560	30.3
Player development	Schedule V	26,756,450	12.5	22,928,403	12.4	22,141,928	13.5	21,947,066	13.9
Team replacement	Schedule VI	29,973,213	12.8	24,973,428	13.5	22,338,013	13.6	23,714,776	15.0
Stadium operations	Schedule VII	37,856,164	16.2	31,957,489	17.2	28,358,094	17.2	27,486,042	17.3
Ticket department, and publicity and promotion	Schedule VIII	18,998,061	8.1	13,915,534	7.5	12,357,060	7.5	11,553,580	7.3
General and administrative	Schedule IX	33,282,113	14.2	26,998,774	14.5	23,027,592	14.0	21,929,760	13.8
Major Leagues Central Fund--Note 1:									
Reimbursement of Commissioner's Office expenses--Note 2		1,026,122	.4	1,163,504	.6	980,975	.6	955,310	.6
Reimbursement of Player Relations Committee		506,236	.2	961,786	.5	419,363	.3	320,224	.2
		233,846,083	100.0	185,610,214	100.0	164,493,683	100.0	158,453,684	100.0
LOSS FROM OPERATIONS		(2,870,739)		(4,669,313)		(3,723,757)		(6,343,154)	
OTHER INCOME (EXPENSE)									
Stadium income from non-baseball activities--net		492,795		589,337		776,866		1,021,771	
Investment income		1,216,108		1,108,833		1,502,924		2,102,651	
Interest expense		(4,267,030)		(4,166,159)		(3,957,017)		(3,868,920)	
Charitable contributions--Note 3		(308,470)							
Miscellaneous--net		1,047,201		2,083,691		412,491		26,046	
		(1,819,396)		(384,298)		(1,264,736)		(718,452)	
LOSS BEFORE INCOME TAXES		$(4,690,135)		$(5,053,611)		$(4,988,493)		$(7,061,606)	

Note 1--Other expenses of the Fund, other than those relating to the Commissioner's Office and the Player Relations Committee, have been included in Schedules III through IX.

Note 2--The Commissioner's Office incurred additional expenses of $652,522 in 1977, $406,858 in 1976, $552,660 in 1975 and $505,739 in 1974 which were covered by its share of World Series ticket sales and other miscellaneous income.

Note 3--Not separately shown for seasons prior to 1977.

See accompanying accountants' letter

COMBINED OPERATING REVENUES (UNAUDITED)

MAJOR LEAGUE BASEBALL

SCHEDULE 11

					Season			
	1977	%	1976	%	1975	%	1974	%
Games receipts:								
Regular season home game receipts, net of admission taxes, visiting club's share, and League shares--Note 1	$122,173,326	52.9	$109,876,921	60.7	$97,779,087	60.8	$92,504,496	60.8
Regular season "away" game receipts	21,781,808	9.4						
All-Star game	467,095	.2	582,512	.3	362,856	.2	394,215	.3
	144,422,229	62.5	110,459,433	61.0	98,141,943	61.0	92,898,711	61.1
Broadcasting and television:								
Games of the Week--regular season	11,170,000	4.8	10,440,000	5.8	8,494,000	5.3	8,379,200	5.5
World Series	9,450,000	4.1	9,430,888	5.2	8,584,000	5.3	8,466,500	5.6
League Championship Series	2,286,000	1.0	1,828,000	1.0	804,250	.5	793,400	.5
All-Star Game	1,104,500	.5	1,004,500	.6	623,925	.4	610,900	.4
Local and regional television--Note 2	17,582,273	7.6	21,004,409	11.6	21,080,341	13.1	17,900,951	11.8
Local and regional radio	7,234,674	3.1						
	48,827,447	21.1	43,707,797	24.2	39,586,516	24.6	36,150,951	23.8
Advertising	3,343,648	1.4	2,776,091	1.5	2,165,865	1.4	2,186,870	1.4
Concessions--net	23,145,129	10.0	15,432,708	8.5	13,496,810	8.4	12,763,471	8.4
Parking--net	3,478,081	1.6	2,828,804	1.6	2,792,805	1.8	2,771,900	1.8
Restaurant or stadium clubs--net	3,377,496	1.5	2,517,989	1.4	2,474,954	1.5	2,390,833	1.6
Royalties and licensing fees--Note 3	597,293	.3						
	33,941,647	14.8	23,555,592	14.8	20,930,434	13.1	20,113,074	13.2
League Champion and World Series:								
Ticket sales, less expenses*	1,705,736	.7	691,749	.4	282,010	.2	1,212,804	.8
Concessions, etc.	1,088,877	.5	775,831	.4	503,774	.3	494,087	.3
	2,794,613	1.2	1,467,580	.8	785,784	.5	1,706,891	1.1
Other operating income	989,408	.4	1,750,499	1.0	1,325,249	.8	1,240,903	.8
TOTAL COMBINED OPERATING REVENUES	$230,975,344	100.0	$180,940,901	100.0	$160,269,926	100.0	$152,110,530	100.0

*Proceeds from ticket sales of League Championship Series and World Series games were distributed as follows:

	1977	1976	1975	1974
Players	$ 2,778,301	$ 2,467,836	$ 1,826,265	$ 2,045,443
Office of the Commissioner	596,823	374,763	507,087	451,078
Leagues	1,079,112	463,836	958,251	677,993
Clubs	2,940,162	1,859,839	1,440,481	1,591,697
	$ 7,394,398	$ 5,166,274	$ 4,732,084	$ 4,766,211
Clubs share above	$ 2,940,162	$ 1,859,839	$ 1,440,481	$ 1,591,697
Less expenses--Note 4	1,234,426	1,168,090	1,158,471	378,893
	$ 1,705,736	$ 691,749	$ 282,010	$ 1,212,804
Number of games played:				
World Series	6	4	7	5
League Championship Series	9	8	6	9
	15	12	13	14

Note 1--Includes "away game receipts" for seasons prior to 1977.

Note 2--Includes local and regional radio for seasons prior to 1977.

Note 3--Not separately shown for seasons prior to 1977.

Note 4--In 1974 one team did not allocate expenses to the League Championship Series and World Series.

See accompanying accountants' letter

COMBINED SPRING TRAINING EXPENSES (UNAUDITED)

MAJOR LEAGUE BASEBALL

SCHEDULE III

	Season			
	1977	1976	1975	1974
Reporting expenses	$ 437,529	$ 376,717	$ 332,956	$ 312,709
"Murphy" and meal money	1,737,128	1,021,012	1,510,396	1,308,290
Hotel and liveout expenses	903,595	588,949	1,004,094	921,118
Home and away game expenses	942,827	470,903	583,873	526,397
Office and club officials expenses	402,518	383,387	369,354	353,884
Publicity and promotion-- Note 1	115,319			
Other expenses	475,129	401,414	571,287	557,610
	5,014,045	3,242,382	4,371,960	3,980,008
Less receipts from spring training games	(2,309,767)	(1,094,248)	(1,819,168)	(1,387,642)
TOTAL COMBINED SPRING TRAINING EXPENSES	$ 2,704,278	$ 2,148,134	$ 2,552,792	$ 2,592,366

Note 1--Not separately shown for seasons prior to 1977

See accompanying accountants' letter

COMBINED TEAM OPERATING EXPENSES (UNAUDITED)

MAJOR LEAGUE BASEBALL

SCHEDULE IV

	Season							
	1977	%*	1976	%*	1975	%*	1974	%*
Salaries:								
Players:								
Current--active major league roster	$47,419,793	20.3	$34,412,397	18.5	$29,915,618	18.2	$26,761,234	16.9
Deferred compensation earned	6,436,535	2.8	1,790,629	1.0	1,180,457	.7	1,151,173	.7
Other, including manager, coaches, trainer, etc.	5,359,821	2.3	4,531,335	2.4	4,187,619	2.5	4,043,570	2.6
	59,216,149	25.4	40,734,361	21.9	35,283,694	21.4	31,955,977	20.2
Workmen's compensation--Note 1	972,706	.4						
Players' Benefit Trust	8,300,000	3.6	8,300,000	4.5	6,450,000	3.9	6,150,000	3.9
Hotels and meals	3,545,772	1.5						
Transportation and road trip expense--Note 2	6,863,322	3.0	8,680,642	4.7	7,900,742	4.8	7,384,044	4.7
Uniforms and playing equipment	723,031	.3	631,118	.3	648,241	.4	587,456	.3
Bats	193,249	.1						
Baseballs--Note 3	718,409	.3	563,117	.3	607,210	.4	554,550	.3
Medical expenses--including team physician, supplies, hospital costs, etc.	569,509	.2	463,459	.2	431,122	.3	440,134	.3
Laundry and clubhouse supplies	331,186	.1	297,697	.2	283,129	.2	269,635	.2
Players moving allowances and expenses--Note 1	315,508	.1						
Umpire development--Note 1	312,000	.1						
Other expenses	682,605	.3	892,768	.5	713,728	.4	612,764	.4
TOTAL COMBINED TEAM OPERATING EXPENSES	$82,743,446	35.4	$60,563,162	32.6	$52,317,866	31.8	$47,954,560	30.3

*Represents the percentage of each item to total operating expenses--$233,846,083 in 1977, $185,610,214 in 1976, $164,493,683 in 1975 and $158,453,684 in 1974 (as shown on page 2).

Note 1--Not separately shown for seasons prior to 1977.

Note 2--Includes "hotels and meals" for seasons prior to 1977.

Note 3--Includes "bats" for seasons prior to 1977.

See accompanying accountants' letter

COMBINED PLAYER DEVELOPMENT EXPENSES (UNAUDITED)

MAJOR LEAGUE BASEBALL

SCHEDULE V

	Season			
	1977	1976	1975	1974
Salaries of farm director, player development director, assistants and other administrative personnel	$ 2,270,881	$ 1,980,594	$ 1,810,094	$ 1,558,263
Salaries of minor league managers, pitching and batting coaches and other instructors	2,276,893	1,325,589	1,141,335	1,071,890
Expenses of minor league managers, pitching and batting coaches and other instructors	370,409	307,749	259,965	255,163
	4,918,183	3,613,932	3,211,394	2,885,316
Player development contract expenses:				
Salaries (including Major League players on option)	10,740,859	10,819,233	10,202,109	10,496,396
Payroll taxes--Note 1	893,859			
Workmen's compensation--Note 1	681,919			
Progress and incentive bonuses	797,536	484,808	518,419	461,695
Transportation home and assignments	768,536	803,835	818,813	797,173
Selection rights and payment	168,835	219,353	350,947	355,345
Uniforms and equipment	214,979	167,446	233,542	300,682
Medical expenses	173,154	156,688	133,289	110,978
Makeup and rookie clubs	536,416	1,126,006	989,283	967,127
Hotels and meals--Note 1	812,258			
Travel and entertainment--Note 1	422,127			
Telephone--Note 1	124,487			
Other	398,629	1,031,910	1,052,589	1,023,985
	16,733,594	14,809,279	14,298,991	14,513,381
Operating losses (net) of owned clubs	954,050	459,746	571,559	510,706
National Association fees	177,505	190,039	172,996	163,432
Winter Instructional League	1,134,923	1,006,180	1,036,604	996,725
Spring training (other than Major League team)	2,616,890	2,106,455	2,085,304	2,129,552
Other expenses	221,305	742,772	765,080	747,954
	5,104,673	4,505,192	4,631,543	4,548,369
TOTAL COMBINED PLAYER DEVELOPMENT EXPENSES	$26,756,450	$22,928,403	$22,141,928	$21,947,066

Note 1--Not separately shown for seasons prior to 1977.

See accompanying accountants' letter

COMBINED TEAM REPLACEMENT COSTS AND EXPENSES (UNAUDITED)

MAJOR LEAGUE BASEBALL

SCHEDULE VI

	Season			
	1977	1976	1975	1974
PLAYER ACQUISITION COSTS				
Clubs that capitalize cost of players contracts--Note 1:				
Amortization of players' contracts:				
Re-entry draft (free agent players)	$ 1,582,402			
All others	9,045,772	$ 8,498,279	$ 5,892,917	$ 4,881,258
Unamortized cost of players' contracts--players released or retired	1,068,359	420,620	426,104	552,061
Drafts and returns--Note 2:				
Loss on contracts acquired and disposed of during year	310,912			
Gain on contracts acquired and disposed of during year	(25,000)			
Net (gain) loss on outright contract sales--Note 3	(1,634,221)	335,856	(58,963)	1,792,184
Amortization of initial roster cost	6,474,712	4,505,478	5,588,195	5,264,083
Clubs on direct write-off method--Note 1:				
Bonuses to players:				
Re-entry draft (free agent players)	672,500			
All others	1,378,315	1,489,555	1,604,132	1,928,331
Sale of contracts	(1,192,920)			
Purchase of contracts--Note 4	1,236,228	(49,670)	(685,552)	(248,242)
College scholarship plan cost	113,837	176,162	180,159	243,579
TOTAL PLAYER ACQUISITION COSTS	19,030,896	15,376,280	12,946,992	14,413,254
SCOUTING EXPENSES				
Salaries	5,350,410	4,433,018	4,260,772	5,203,506
Travel	3,829,374	3,213,067	3,133,827	3,630,914
Major League Scouting Bureau	1,693,053	1,828,664	1,796,647	267,014
Other	69,480	122,399	199,775	200,088
TOTAL SCOUTING EXPENSES	10,942,317	9,597,148	9,391,021	9,301,522
TOTAL COMBINED TEAM REPLACEMENT COSTS AND EXPENSES	$29,973,213	$24,973,428	$22,338,013	$23,714,776
Note 1--Number of clubs that capitalized the cost of players' contracts	19	18	16	17
Number of clubs on the direct write-off method	7	6	8	7

Note 2--Not separately shown for seasons prior to 1977.

Note 3--Includes $156,658 loss in 1977; gross amounts not available prior to 1977.

Note 4--Includes "(sale) of contracts" for seasons prior to 1977.

See accompanying accountants' letter

COMBINED STADIUM OPERATIONS EXPENSES (UNAUDITED)

MAJOR LEAGUE BASEBALL

SCHEDULE VII

	Season			
	1977	1976	1975	1974
Salaries--including ushers, grounds crews, cleaning personnel, etc.	$14,441,271	$12,435,291	$11,926,812	$11,271,429
Uniforms and laundry--Note 1	142,914			
Wages of ticket sellers for "day of game only"	1,216,404	893,606	802,888	811,693
Security service--outside gate	550,525	658,563	477,618	441,578
Rent	9,198,776	6,972,763	5,896,678	5,870,743
Light, heat, and power	2,549,041	2,092,642	1,663,161	1,415,103
Maintenance and repairs	2,580,217	2,420,280	2,032,674	1,994,523
Property taxes	1,841,664	1,769,212	1,557,762	1,609,992
Depreciation and amortization	3,046,230	3,139,849	2,522,653	2,635,582
Playing field maintenance	232,026	328,403	437,039	429,523
Medical service--Note 1	128,423			
Music related expenses--Note 1	177,753			
Rubbish removal--Note 1	687,158			
Other expenses	1,063,762	1,246,880	1,040,809	1,005,876
TOTAL COMBINED STADIUM OPERATIONS EXPENSES	$37,856,164	$31,957,489	$28,358,094	$27,486,042

Note 1--Not separately shown for seasons prior to 1977.

See accompanying accountants' letter

COMBINED TICKET DEPARTMENT, AND PUBLICITY
AND PROMOTION EXPENSES (UNAUDITED)

MAJOR LEAGUE BASEBALL

SCHEDULE VIII

	Season			
	1977	1976	1975	1974
Ticket department:				
Salaries (excluding "day of game only" personnel)	$ 3,869,903	$ 2,880,465	$ 2,553,967	$ 2,442,285
Rent and other expenses	225,931	276,162	177,136	196,784
Ticket printing and schedules	1,259,540	1,152,585	1,137,248	1,063,423
Sales commissions--Note 1	475,283			
Travel and reimbursed expenses--Note 1	120,586			
Postage, armored car services and other related expenses	891,966	811,144	734,555	670,818
TOTAL COMBINED TICKET DEPARTMENT EXPENSES	6,843,209	5,120,356	4,602,906	4,373,310
Publicity and promotion:				
Salaries	2,324,681	1,793,534	1,708,624	1,573,131
Travel and reimbursed expenses	346,510	251,679	235,669	228,440
Press room expenses	945,686	833,012	851,218	847,947
Special events	4,202,467	2,964,935	2,523,260	2,225,917
Advertising--Note 1	2,937,459			
Promotional films--Note 1	154,271			
Press guide--Note 1	216,594			
Dinners and testimonials--Note 1	180,916			
Other expenses	846,268	2,952,018	2,435,383	2,304,835
TOTAL COMBINED PUBLICITY AND PROMOTION EXPENSES	12,154,852	8,795,178	7,754,154	7,180,270
TOTAL COMBINED TICKET DEPARTMENT, AND PUBLICITY AND PROMOTION EXPENSES	$18,998,061	$13,915,534	$12,357,060	$11,553,580

Note 1--Not separately shown for seasons prior to 1977.

See accompanying accountants' letter

COMBINED GENERAL AND ADMINISTRATIVE EXPENSES (UNAUDITED)

MAJOR LEAGUE BASEBALL

SCHEDULE IX

	Season			
	1977	1976	1975	1974
Salaries	$ 8,556,796	$ 6,596,743	$ 6,283,973	$ 5,969,391
Payroll taxes	3,856,537	4,011,825	3,434,994	3,276,618
Workmen's compensation--Note 1	547,844			
Non-player benefits--including health, life and disability insurance, profit sharing and pension plans	3,123,778	2,670,780	2,728,616	2,482,102
Travel and entertainment	1,624,455	1,437,055	1,248,582	1,350,012
Office rent, light, heat--Note 1	201,554			
Telephone	1,635,723	1,437,098	1,241,723	1,099,728
Audit	742,916			
Legal--Note 2	2,328,038	2,820,267	1,996,774	1,858,214
Other professional services-- Note 1	454,258			
Business taxes	643,791	570,369	677,894	729,316
Insurance--including liability, team travel and disaster, fire, and other	4,068,355	2,866,142	2,129,443	1,854,861
Postage	499,272	448,134	310,557	325,757
Stationery, printing and office supplies	820,078	643,504	580,963	534,664
Depreciation and amortization-- other than stadium and players' contracts	1,580,405	1,422,222	546,035	580,219
Dues and subscriptions--Note 1	147,856			
Computer services--Note 1	245,011			
Office rental and repairs-- Note 1	207,676			
Office cleaning--Note 1	90,370			
Contributions (Major Leagues Central Fund only)	416,333	406,833	383,500	333,500
Bad debts--Note 1	137,651			
Other expenses	1,353,416	1,667,802	1,464,538	1,535,378
TOTAL COMBINED GENERAL AND ADMINISTRATIVE EXPENSES	$33,282,113	$26,998,774	$23,027,592	$21,929,760

Note 1--Not separately shown for seasons prior to 1977.

Note 2--Includes "audit" for seasons prior to 1977.

See accompanying accountants' letter

Appendix E: Summary Tabulations of the Clubs' Financial Survey for the 1979 Season

A number of new items are tabulated in this survey that were not included in earlier years. Also, minor changes have been made in the definitions of some items. Most such changes are noted in the footnotes to the tables.

Certain Financial Data (Unaudited)

MAJOR LEAGUE BASEBALL

1979, 1978, 1977, 1976 and 1975 Seasons

Accountants' Letter
Combined Summary of Operations (Before Income Taxes)
Combined Summary of Operating Revenues
Combined Spring Training Expenses
Combined Team Operating Expenses
Combined Player Development Expenses
Combined Team Replacement Costs and Expenses
Combined Stadium Operations Expenses
Combined Ticket Department, and Publicity and
   Promotion Expenses
Combined General and Administrative Expenses

Ernst & Whinney

153 East 53rd Street
New York, New York 10022

212/888-9100

December 2, 1980

Baseball - Office of the Commissioner
15 West 51th Street
New York, New York

Gentlemen:

At your request, we have corresponded with each of the major league
baseball clubs requesting that certain financial data be furnished to
us. The accompanying combined summaries of operations (before income
taxes) and operating revenues, as compiled by us, reflect a
summarization of such data for the 1979, 1978, 1977, 1976, and 1975
seasons, and, as requested, also include the income and expenses of the
Major Leagues Central Fund for each of the five years ended October 31,
1979. The accompanying related schedules of combined spring training
expenses, team operating expenses, player development expenses, team
replacement costs and expenses, stadium operations expenses, ticket
department, and publicity and promotion expenses, and general and
administrative expenses, as compiled by us, reflect a summarization of
such data as furnished to us for the 1979 and 1978 seasons only.

The accounting for players' contract costs differs among the individual
clubs, and there may be other existing differences in accounting
principles and practices. In addition, although certain
reclassifications and combinations have been made to various expense
categories as submitted by the individual clubs, other inconsistencies
in account classifications may still exist. Accordingly, the reader or
user of the accompanying financial summaries and schedules should
consider these matters in interpreting the data shown therein.

We have not audited or reviewed the accompanying summaries, related
schedules or data, other than the income and expenses of the Major
Leagues Central Fund, and, accordingly, we are unable to and do not
express an opinion or any other form of assurance on them.

Very truly yours,

Ernst & Whinney

COMBINED SUMMARY OF OPERATIONS (BEFORE INCOME TAXES) (UNAUDITED)

MAJOR LEAGUE BASEBALL

SCHEDULE I

	Schedule		1979	%	1978	%	1977 (Season)	%	1976	%	1975	%
OPERATING REVENUES, including receipts of Major Leagues Central Fund	Schedule	II	$301,750,111		$265,308,026		$233,285,111		$182,035,149		$162,589,094	
OPERATING EXPENSES												
Spring training	Schedule	III	5,890,282	1.9	5,511,943	2.1	5,014,045	2.1	3,242,382	1.7	4,371,960	2.6
Team	Schedule	IV	118,724,043	39.3	97,705,914	36.8	82,743,446	35.0	60,563,162	32.4	52,317,866	31.5
Player development	Schedule	V	33,421,672	11.1	29,039,742	11.0	26,756,450	11.3	22,928,403	12.3	22,141,928	13.3
Team replacement	Schedule	VI	35,491,486	11.7	34,956,769	13.2	29,660,229	12.6	24,973,428	13.4	22,338,013	13.4
Stadium operations	Schedule	VII	45,552,475	15.1	41,593,659	15.7	37,856,164	16.1	31,957,489	17.1	28,358,094	17.0
Ticket department, publicity and promotion	Schedule	VIII	22,397,648	7.4	19,437,641	7.3	18,998,061	8.1	13,915,534	7.5	12,357,060	7.4
General and administrative	Schedule	IX	38,831,433	12.8	35,395,110	13.3	33,595,097	14.2	26,998,774	14.5	23,027,592	13.9
Major Leagues Central Fund--Note 1: Reimbursement of Commissioner's Office expenses--Note 2			1,259,633	.4	1,108,428	.4	1,026,122	.4	1,163,504	.6	980,975	.6
Reimbursement of Player Relations Committee			794,608	.3	554,234	.2	506,236	.2	961,736	.5	419,363	.3
			302,363,300	100.0	265,303,440	100.0	236,155,850	100.0	186,704,452	100.0	166,312,851	100.0
PROFIT (LOSS) FROM OPERATION			(613,189)		4,586		(2,870,739)		(4,669,313)		(3,723,757)	
OTHER INCOME (EXPENSE)												
Stadium income from non-baseball activities--net			1,205,911		1,030,267		492,795		589,337		776,866	
Investment income			3,529,307		2,145,982		1,216,108		1,108,833		1,502,924	
Interest expense			(5,368,839)		(4,271,645)		(4,267,030)		(4,166,159)		(3,957,017)	
Charitable contributions--Note 3			(483,142)		(293,137)		(308,470)					
Miscellaneous--net			756,431		(50,976)		1,047,201		2,083,691		412,491	
			(360,332)		(1,439,509)		(1,819,396)		(384,298)		(1,264,736)	
LOSS BEFORE INCOME TAXES			$ (973,521)		$ (1,434,923)		$ (4,690,135)		$ (5,053,611)		$ (4,988,493)	

Note 1--Other expenses of the Fund, other than those relating to the Commissioner's Office and the Player Relations Committee, have been included in Schedules III through IX.

Note 2--The Commissioner's Office incurred additional expenses of $912,460 in 1979, $766,422 in 1978, $652,522 in 1977, $406,858 in 1976 and $552,660 in 1975 which were covered by its share of World Series ticket sales and other miscellaneous income.

Note 3--Not separately shown for seasons prior to 1977.

See accompanying accountants' letter

COMBINED SUMMARY OF OPERATING REVENUES (UNAUDITED)

MAJOR LEAGUE BASEBALL

SCHEDULE II

	1979	%	1978	%	1977	%	1976	%	1975	%
Season										
Games receipts:										
Regular season home game receipts, net of admission taxes, visiting club's share, and League shares--Note 1	$156,542,625	51.9	$140,035,564	52.8	$122,173,326	52.4	$109,876,921	60.4	$97,779,087	60.2
Regular season "away" game receipts--Note 2	26,983,815	8.9	24,227,461	9.1	21,781,808	9.3				
Unredeemed tickets, rain checks, etc.--Note 2	1,195,525	.4	974,951	.4						
All-Star game	416,723	.1	468,359	.2	467,095	.2	582,512	.3	362,856	.2
Receipts from exhibition games	2,929,746	1.0	2,522,366	.9	2,309,767	1.0	1,094,248	.6	1,819,168	1.1
	188,068,434	62.3	168,228,701	63.4	146,731,996	62.9	111,553,681	61.3	99,961,111	61.5
Broadcasting and television:										
Games of the Week--regular season	12,895,000	4.3	11,245,000	4.3	11,170,000	4.8	10,440,000	5.7	8,494,000	5.2
World Series	10,845,000	3.6	9,662,750	3.6	9,450,000	4.0	9,430,888	5.2	8,584,000	5.3
League Championship Series	2,950,000	1.0	2,471,750	.9	2,286,000	1.0	1,828,000	1.0	804,250	.5
All-Star Game	1,322,500	.4	1,220,500	.5	1,104,500	.5	1,004,500	.6	623,925	.4
Local and regional television--Note 3	23,732,065	7.9	18,586,502	7.0	16,494,582	7.0	21,004,409	11.5	21,080,341	13.0
Local and regional radio	11,337,365	3.8	9,565,578	3.6	8,322,365	3.6				
	63,081,930	21.0	52,752,080	19.9	48,827,447	20.9	43,707,797	24.0	39,586,516	24.4
Advertising	4,517,477	1.5	3,699,687	1.4	3,343,648	1.4	2,776,091	1.5	2,165,865	1.3
Concessions--net	33,177,937	11.0	27,184,243	10.3	23,145,129	9.9	15,432,708	8.5	13,496,810	8.3
Parking--net	4,325,506	1.4	4,576,186	1.7	3,478,081	1.5	2,828,804	1.5	2,792,805	1.7
Restaurant or stadium clubs--net	3,954,909	1.3	4,170,245	1.6	3,377,496	1.5	2,517,989	1.4	2,474,954	1.5
Royalties and licensing fees--Note 4	485,152	.2	597,214	.2	597,293	.3				
	40,460,981	15.4	40,227,575	15.2	33,941,647	14.6	23,555,592	12.9	20,930,434	12.8
League Championship and World Series:										
Ticket sales, less expenses*	641,650	.2	1,925,387	.7	1,705,736	.7	691,749	.4	282,010	.2
Concessions, etc.	1,575,204	.5	1,426,827	.5	1,088,877	.5	775,831	.4	503,774	.3
	2,216,854	.7	3,352,214	1.2	2,794,613	1.2	1,467,580	.8	785,784	.5
Other operating income	1,921,912	.6	747,456	.3	989,408	.4	1,750,499	1.0	1,325,249	.8
TOTAL COMBINED OPERATING REVENUES	$301,750,111	100.0	$265,308,026	100.0	$233,285,111	100.0	$182,035,149	100.0	$162,589,094	100.0
*Proceeds from ticket sales of League Championship Series and World Series games were distributed as follows:										
Players	$ 2,654,824		$ 3,301,934		$ 2,778,301		$ 2,467,836		$ 1,826,265	
Office of the Commissioner	658,615		697,325		596,823		374,763		507,087	
Leagues	1,255,590		1,216,148		1,079,112		463,836		958,251	
Clubs	2,709,121		3,328,727		2,940,162		1,859,839		1,440,481	
	$ 7,278,150		$ 8,544,334		$ 7,394,398		$ 5,166,274		$ 4,732,084	
Clubs share above	$ 2,709,121		$ 3,328,727		$ 2,940,162		$ 1,859,839		$ 1,440,481	
Less expenses	2,097,471		1,403,340		1,234,426		1,168,090		1,158,471	
	$ 641,650		$ 1,925,387		$ 1,705,736		$ 691,749		$ 282,010	
Number of games played:										
World Series	7		6		6		4		7	
League Championship Series	7		8		9		8		6	
	14		14		15		12		13	

Note 1--Includes "away game receipts" for seasons prior to 1977.
Note 2--Not separately shown for seasons prior to 1978.
Note 3--Includes local and regional radio for seasons prior to 1977.
Note 4--Not separately shown for seasons prior to 1977.

See accompanying accountants' letter

COMBINED SPRING TRAINING EXPENSES (UNAUDITED)

MAJOR LEAGUE BASEBALL

SCHEDULE III

	Season	
	1979	1978
Reporting expenses	$ 507,553	$ 530,712
"Murphy" and meal money	2,037,124	1,823,517
Hotel and liveout expenses	1,183,158	1,038,595
Home and away game expenses	663,474	698,929
Office and club officials expenses	478,728	429,231
Publicity and promotion	133,408	124,053
Playing equipment (baseballs, bats, uniforms, etc.)	240,063	252,122
Laundry	62,248	63,218
Medical fees and expenses	127,274	110,008
Other expenses	457,252	441,558
TOTAL COMBINED SPRING TRAINING EXPENSES	$5,890,282	$5,511,943

See accompanying accountants' letter

COMBINED TEAM OPERATING EXPENSES (UNAUDITED)

MAJOR LEAGUE BASEBALL

SCHEDULE IV

	Season			
	1979	%*	1978	%*
Salaries:				
Players:				
Current--active major league roster:				
Re-entry draft	$ 7,000,759	2.3	$ 4,207,070	1.6
All others	68,836,347	22.8	55,662,981	21.0
	75,837,106	25.1	59,870,051	22.6
Deferred compensation earned:				
Re-entry draft	1,071,889	.3	657,728	.3
All others	7,523,377	2.5	5,933,428	2.2
	8,595,266	2.8	6,591,156	2.5
Manager, coaches, trainer, etc.	5,796,903	1.9	5,516,915	2.1
Clubhouse salaries	597,971	.2	460,077	.2
Other salaries	834,604	.3	405,743	.1
	91,661,850	30.3	72,843,942	27.5
Workmen's compensation	1,195,122	.4	1,067,290	.4
Players' Benefit Trust	8,300,000	2.7	8,300,000	3.1
Hotels and meals	4,180,809	1.4	3,941,490	1.5
Transportation and road trip expense	7,767,919	2.6	6,747,338	2.5
Uniforms and playing equipment	791,095	.3	672,907	.2
Clubhouse expenses	614,223	.2	138,465	.1
Bats	222,349	.1	187,856	.1
Baseballs	748,421	.2	715,621	.3
Medical expenses--including team physicians, supplies, hospital cost, etc.	766,967	.3	676,109	.2
Players' moving allowances and expenses	268,386	.1	279,583	.1
Insurance (life, accident, team travel, disaster, etc.)	1,279,225	.4	959,906	.4
Umpire development	234,480	.1	338,000	.1
Other expenses	693,197	.2	837,407	.3
TOTAL COMBINED TEAM OPERATING EXPENSES	$118,724,043	39.3	$97,705,914	36.8

*Represents the percentage of each item to total operating expenses--$302,363,300 in 1979, and $265,303,440 in 1978 (as shown on page 2).

See accompanying accountants' letter

COMBINED PLAYER DEVELOPMENT EXPENSES (UNAUDITED)

MAJOR LEAGUE BASEBALL

SCHEDULE V

	Season	
	1979	1978
Salaries of farm director, player development director, assistants and other administrative personnel	$ 2,354,657	$ 1,999,006
Salaries of minor league managers, pitching and batting coaches and other instructors	3,180,493	2,842,092
Expenses of farm director, minor league managers, pitching and batting coaches and other instructors	1,102,167	918,130
	6,637,317	5,759,228
Player development contract expenses:		
Salaries (including Major League players on option)	12,798,993	12,120,149
Payroll taxes	1,084,815	1,041,349
Workmen's compensation	687,504	522,969
Progress and incentive bonuses	634,538	631,957
Transportation home and assignments	827,234	808,399
Selection rights and payment	160,019	142,780
Uniforms and equipment	256,043	242,136
Medical expenses	309,376	231,802
Makeup and rookie clubs	1,431,254	828,438
Hotels and meals	1,329,393	967,047
Travel and entertainment	290,694	212,279
Telephone	175,606	161,971
	19,985,469	17,911,276
Operating losses (net) of owned clubs	909,483	559,004
National Association fees	300,224	243,446
Winter Instructional League	1,523,210	1,281,894
Spring training (other than Major League team)	3,108,471	2,535,824
Other expenses	957,498	749,070
	6,798,886	5,369,238
TOTAL COMBINED PLAYER DEVELOPMENT EXPENSES	$33,421,672	$29,039,742

See accompanying accountants' letter

COMBINED TEAM REPLACEMENT COSTS AND EXPENSES (UNAUDITED)

MAJOR LEAGUE BASEBALL

SCHEDULE VI

	Season	
	1979	1978
PLAYER ACQUISITION COSTS		
Clubs that capitalize cost of players' contracts--Note 1:		
Amortization of players' contracts:		
Re-entry draft (free agent players)	$ 1,768,212	$ 826,480
First year players' bonuses (high school, college, or minor league players who are not on a major league contract)	3,226,940	4,534,255
Contracts acquired from other clubs	884,992	1,963,656
Contracts renegotiated	755,575	786,067
All others	5,152,570	4,105,791
	11,788,289	12,216,249
Unamortized cost of players' contracts-- players released or retired	1,083,377	1,787,190
Drafts and returns--net loss on contracts acquired and disposed of during year	296,020	13,750
Net (gain) on outright contract sales	(1,906,120)	(1,239,601)
Amortization of initial roster cost	8,416,645	7,503,433
Clubs on direct write-off method--Note 1:		
Bonuses to players:		
Re-entry draft (free agent players)	597,188	982,763
Rookies and all others (high school, college, or minor league players who are not on a major league contract)	2,151,515	1,585,708
Sale of contracts	(762,647)	(650,865)
Purchase of contracts	737,001	842,993
College scholarship plan cost	95,180	102,564
TOTAL PLAYER ACQUISITION COSTS	22,496,448	23,144,184
SCOUTING EXPENSES		
Salaries	6,279,644	5,771,270
Travel	4,931,214	4,321,171
Major League Scouting Bureau	1,646,054	1,588,758
Try-out camps	126,707	120,026
Other	11,419	11,360
TOTAL SCOUTING EXPENSES	12,995,038	11,812,585
TOTAL COMBINED TEAM REPLACEMENT COSTS AND EXPENSES	$35,491,486	$34,956,769
Note 1--Number of clubs that capitalized the cost of players' contracts	19	19
Number of clubs on the direct write-off method	7	7

See accompanying accountants' letter

COMBINED STADIUM OPERATIONS EXPENSES (UNA⌐

MAJOR LEAGUE BASEBALL

SCHEDULE VII

	Season	
	1979	1978
Salaries--including ushers, grounds crews, cleaning personnel, etc.	$16,601,776	$14,996,807
Uniforms and laundry	183,795	179,478
Wages of ticket sellers for "day of game only"	1,200,711	1,174,912
Security service--outside gate	492,480	452,296
Security service--inside gate (including closed circuit T.V.)	1,361,893	1,410,736
Rent	12,772,619	10,987,118
Light, heat, and power	3,132,981	2,851,050
Maintenance and repairs	2,725,201	2,493,611
Property taxes	1,307,084	1,755,071
Depreciation and amortization	3,526,118	2,960,734
Playing field maintenance	298,125	310,797
Medical service	190,892	179,914
Music related expenses	256,404	254,401
Rubbish removal	597,480	801,674
Permits for amusements, licenses, etc.	101,663	84,873
Other expenses	803,253	700,187
TOTAL COMBINED STADIUM OPERATIONS EXPENSES	$45,552,475	$41,593,659

See accompanying accountants' letter

COMBINED TICKET DEPARTMENT, AND PUBLICITY
AND PROMOTION EXPENSES (UNAUDITED)

MAJOR LEAGUE BASEBALL

SCHEDULE VIII

	Season	
	1979	1978
Ticket department:		
Salaries (excluding "day of game only" personnel)	$ 4,719,231	$ 4,211,435
Rent and other expenses	235,621	169,846
Ticket printing and schedules	1,420,256	1,236,378
Sales commissions	583,215	476,709
Travel and reimbursed expenses	112,427	96,280
Postage (including direct mailing costs)	363,967	216,565
Office supplies	211,296	164,086
Other expenses	756,384	567,326
TOTAL COMBINED TICKET DEPARTMENT EXPENSES	8,402,397	7,138,625
Publicity and promotion:		
Salaries	2,887,635	2,665,006
Travel and reimbursed expenses	279,794	267,920
Press room expenses	1,003,344	1,072,976
Special events	4,323,634	4,053,945
	8,494,407	8,059,847
Media:		
Advertising	2,978,598	1,980,901
Promotional films	104,994	105,552
Press guide	211,753	202,034
Photography and related costs	325,848	252,943
Club newsletter, leaflets, etc.	638,679	533,827
Player appearance expenses	144,306	154,858
Professional fees	112,382	343,034
	4,516,560	3,573,149
Dinners and testimonials	142,280	111,910
Other expenses	842,004	554,110
TOTAL COMBINED PUBLICITY AND PROMOTION EXPENSES	13,995,251	12,299,016
TOTAL COMBINED TICKET DEPARTMENT, PUBLICITY AND PROMOTION EXPENSES	$22,397,648	$19,437,641

See accompanying accountants' letter

COMBINED GENERAL AND ADMINISTRATIVE EXPENSES (UNAUDITED)

MAJOR LEAGUE BASEBALL

SCHEDULE IX

	Season	
	1979	1978
Salaries	$10,328,790	$ 8,812,735
Payroll taxes	5,237,745	4,357,618
Workmen's compensation	615,175	467,924
Non-player benefits--including health, life and disability insurance, profit sharing and pension plans	3,938,789	3,579,817
Travel and entertainment	1,855,196	1,797,087
Office rent, light, heat	157,056	184,634
Telephone	1,870,393	1,706,764
Audit	880,399	815,884
Legal	2,373,545	1,852,289
Other professional services	604,982	475,645
Business taxes	605,034	623,960
Insurance:		
General liability	2,634,330	3,146,176
Excess liability	912,152	865,607
Fire and all other	1,088,619	1,043,020
	4,635,101	5,054,803
Postage	562,054	504,308
Stationery, printing and office supplies	734,399	688,263
Depreciation and amortization--other than stadium and players' contracts	1,713,130	2,137,232
Cafeteria and dining room	281,506	190,052
Dues and subscriptions	149,562	131,803
Computer services	314,170	243,119
Office rental and repairs	212,318	215,452
Office cleaning	105,485	82,878
Contributions (Major Leagues Central Fund only)	487,000	463,086
Bad debts	198,925	122,755
Other expenses	970,679	887,002
TOTAL COMBINED GENERAL AND ADMINISTRATIVE EXPENSES	$38,831,433	$35,395,110

See accompanying accountants' letter

Bibliography

Books, Reports, Government Publications, and Theses

American Enterprise Institute. "Pro Sports: Should Government Intervene?" Panel discussion, American Enterprise Institute for Public Policy Research, Washington, February 22, 1977.

American League of Professional Baseball Clubs. *American League Red Book.* Los Angeles: M.G. Book Graphics, 1978.

American League of Professional Baseball Clubs. *Annual Report.* Various years. (Supplied by the American League Office.)

Ball, Donald W., and Loy, John W., eds. *Sport and the Social Order: Contributions to the Sociology of Sport.* Reading, Ma.: Addison-Wesley Publishing Co., 1975.

Baseball Blue Book, 1978. St. Petersburg, Fla.: Baseball Blue Book, Inc., 1978.

Baseball Commissioner's Office. Audited financial statements of the Major Leagues Central Fund. Various years. Also, audited financial statements of the League Championship Series and World Series Fund. Various years.

The Baseball Encyclopedia. New York: The Macmillan Co., Inc., 1976.

Cain, William O. "Bayesian Discrete Optimizing as an Approach to a Scheduling Problem: Major League Baseball." D.B.A. thesis, Harvard Business School, 1972.

Demmert, Henry G. *The Economics of Professional League Sports,* Lexington, Ma.: D.C. Heath & Co., 1973.

The Final Report of the President's Commission on Olympic Sports, 1975-1977, vols. 1 and 2. Washington: USGPO, 1977.

Ford, William T., and Houdek, Frank G. "Sports and the Law: A Bibliography." Los Angeles: Los Angeles County Law Library, May 1976.

Gallagher, Daniel J. "An Economic Analysis of the Player Reservation System in the Professional Team Sports Industry in the United States." Ph.D. thesis, University of Maryland, 1976.

Gebhard, Theodore Alan. "A Pricing-Output Optimization Model for a Professional Team Sports League." Ph.D. thesis, University of Illinois, 1975.

Hollander, Zander. *The Modern Encyclopedia of Basketball.* New York: Four Winds Press, 1973.

Koppett, Leonard. *A Thinking Man's Guide to Baseball.* New York: E.P. Dutton & Co., Inc., 1967.

Kowett, Don. *The Rich Who Own Sports.* New York: Random House, 1977.

Lieberman Research, Inc. "How Sports Fans Feel about Baseball: An Attitudinal and Motivational Investigation." Report of Lieberman Research Inc. for the Major League Baseball Promotion Corporation, August 1973. (Received from the Baseball Commissioner's Office.)

Loy, John W. Jr., and Kenyon, Gerald S. *Sport, Culture, and Society.* New York: The Macmillan Co., Inc., 1957.

Major League Baseball Player Relations Committee, Inc. *Basic Players Agreement, 1976-1979* and *Basic Players Agreement, 1973.*

Markham, Jesse W. *The American Economy.* New York: George Braziller, 1963.

Minor League Digest. St. Petersburg, Fla.: Baseball Blue Book, Inc., 1977.

National Association Highlights, 29th ed. St. Petersburg, Fla. National Association of Professional Baseball Leagues, February 1977.

National League of Professional Baseball Clubs. *Annual Report.* Various years. (Supplied by the National League Office.)

National League of Professional Baseball Clubs. *National League Green Book.* Los Angeles: M.G. Book Graphics, 1978.

Noll, Roger G., ed. *Government and the Sports Business.* Washington: The Brookings Institution, 1974.

Noll, Roger G. "Major League Team Sports." *The Structure of American Industry,* 5th ed. Edited by Walter Adams. New York: The Macmillan Co., Inc., 1977.

Official 1978 Baseball Guide. St. Louis, Mo.: The Sporting News, 1978.

Pigou, Arthur C. *The Economics of Welfare,* 4th ed. London: Macmillan & Co., Ltd., 1952.

Pittsburgh Area Chamber of Commerce. "The Impact of Baseball on the Pittsburgh Economy." Pittsburgh Area Chamber of Commerce, 1977.

Ross, Gary N. "Essays on the Economics of the Professional Team Sports Industry." Ph.D. diss., The City University of New York, 1974.

Seymour, Harold. *Baseball: The Early Years.* New York: Oxford University Press, 1960.

Shannon, Bill, and Kalinsky, George. *The Ballparks.* New York: Hawthorn Books, 1975.

Sindlinger's Economic Service. "Sports Participation Report," August 15, 1976.

Sobel, Lionel S. *Professional Sports and the Law.* New York: Law-Arts Publishers, Inc., 1977.

Sports Business. Various issues. Dayton, N.J.: The M.A.R.S. Corportion, semimonthly.

Stocking, George W., and Watkins, Roger. *Cartels in Action.* New York: Twentieth Century Fund, 1946.

Styer, Robert A. *The Encyclopedia of Hockey.* New York: A.S. Barnes and Company, 1973.

Treat, Roger. *The Encyclopedia of Football.* New York: A.S. Barnes and
    Company, 1975.
U.S. Congress, House, Select Committee on Professional Sports, *Inquiry
    into Professional Sports, Hearings.* Parts 1 and 2, 94th Cong., 2d sess.
    Washington: USGPO, 1976.
U.S., Congress, Senate, Committee on the Judiciary. Subcommittee on
    Antitrust and Monopoly. *Professional Basketball, Hearings.* Parts 1
    and 2, 92d Cong., 1st sess. Washington: USGPO, 1972.
U.S. Department of Interior, Bureau of Outdoor Recreation. *Outdoor
    Recreation: A Legacy for America.* Washington: USGPO, 1973.
U.S. Department of Justice. Task Group on Antitrust Immunities. *Report.*
    January 1977.

Articles

Angell, Roger. "The Sporting Scene: Cast a Cold Eye." *The New Yorker,*
    November 22, 1976, p. 151.
Athey, Thomas H. "Can You Buy a Pennant?" Unpublished paper.
    Pomona, Calif.: School of Business Administration, Information
    Systems Department, January 1978.
"The Balance of Power in Professional Sports." *Maine Law Review,*
    February 1970, pp. 459-480.
"Baseball's Opposition to Provisions of H.R. 10612 Affecting Professional
    Sports." *Inquiry into Professional Sports.* Hearings before the House
    Select Committee on Professional Sports, 94th Cong., 2d sess., pt. 1,
    pp. 17-20. Washington: USGPO, 1976.
Blum, Marc P. "Valuing Intangibles: What Are the Choices for Valuing
    Professional Sports Teams?" *The Journal of Taxation,* November
    1976, pp. 286-288.
Burck, Charles G. "Why the Sports Business Ain't What It Used to Be."
    Fortune, May 1977, p. 295.
Carlson, Robert S. "The Business of Professional Sports: A Reexamination
    in Progress." *New York Law Forum* 18 (1973):915.
Daly, George, and Moore, William J. "Alternative Property Right Assign-
    ments and the Allocation of Resources; The Player Draft, the Reserve
    Clause, and Competition in Major League Baseball," forthcoming in
    Economic Inquiry, journal of the Western Economic Association,
    spring 1981.
Dworkin, James B. "The Impact of Final-Offer Interest Arbitration on
    Bargaining: The Case of Major League Baseball." Industrial Relations
    Research Association Series. *Proceedings of the Twenty-Ninth Annual
    Winter Meeting.* Atlantic City, N.J., 1976, pp. 161-169.

El-Hodiri, Mohamed, and Quirk, James. "An Economic Model of a Professional Sports League." *Journal of Political Economy* 79 (November/December 1971):1302-1319.

Grella, George. "Baseball and the American Dream." *Eastern Review,* April 1977, p. 39. Reprinted from *Massachusetts Review,* 1975.

Hertzberg, Hendrick. "Down in the Minors." *The New Yorker,* October 6, 1975, p. 46.

Hochberg, Philip R. "Second and Goal to Go: The Legislative Attack in the 92nd Congress on Sports Broadcasting Practices." *New York Law Forum* 18 (1973):135.

Hochberg, Philip, and Horowitz, Ira. "Broadcasting and CATV: The Beauty and the Bane of Major College Football." *Law and Contemporary Problems,* 38 (1973):112.

Jones, J.C.H. "The Economics of the National Hockey League." *Canadian Journal of Economics,* January/February 1969, pp. 1-20.

Kennedy, Ray, and Williamson, Nancy. "Money: The Monster Threatening Sports," pt. 1. *Sports Illustrated,* July 17, 1978, pp. 29-88.

_____ . "Money: The Monster Threatening Sports," pt. 2. *Sports Illustrated,* July 24, 1978, pp. 34-49.

Klinger, Leslie, S. "Tax Aspects of Buying, Selling and Owning Professional Sports Teams. " *Los Angeles Bar Bulletin,* March 1973, pp. 162-180.

Koch, James V. "A Troubled Cartel: The NCAA." *Law and Contemporary Problems* 38 (1973):135.

Koppett, Leonard. "Sports and the Law: An Overview." *New York Law Forum* 18 (1973):815.

_____ . "A Strange Business Baseball." *New York Times Magazine,* September 2, 1973, p. 10.

Levick, Marsha. "Tying Arrangements in the Sale of Season Tickets." *Temple Law Quarterly* 47 (1974):761.

Lowell, Cym H. "Collective Bargaining in the Professional Team Sport Industry." *Law and Contemporary Problems* 38 (1973):3.

Meran, Harry B. "The Sale of Minor League Baseball Players during Liquidation—The Application of *Corn Products* to Depreciable Property." *Temple Law Quarterly* 45 (1972):291.

Meyer, Philip E. "Human Assets Accounting in the Professional Sports Industry." *The CPA Journal,* May 1973, pp. 417-419.

Mogull, Robert G. "Football Salaries and Race: Some Empirical Evidence." *Industrial Relations,* February 1973, pp. 109-112.

Neale, Walter C. "The Peculiar Economics of Professional Sports." *The Quarterly Journal of Economics,* February 1964, pp. 1-14.

"Old, New Sponsors Follow Audience Upsurge." *Television/Radio Age,* January 31, 1977, p. 29.

Quirk, James. "An Economic Analysis of Team Movements in Professional Sports." *Law and Contemporary Problems* 38 (1973):42.

Reisner, Carl L. "Tackling Intercollegiate Athletics: Antitrust Analysis." *Yale Law Journal* 87 (1978):655.

Rivett, Patrick. "The Structure of League Football." *Operational Research Quarterly,* December 1975, pp. 801-812.

Roberts, Michael, "Balls and Chains." *The New Republic,* February 1, 1975, pp. 9-10.

Rottenberg, Simon. "The Baseball Players' Labor Market." *Journal of Political Economy,* June 1956, pp. 242-258.

Schneiderman, Michael. "Professional Sport. Involuntary Servitude and the Popular Will." *Gonzaga Law Review* 7 (1971):63.

Schwartz, Barry, and Barsky, Stephen F. "The Home Advantage." *Social Forces,* March 1977, pp. 641-661.

Scoville, James G. "Wage Determination and the Development of Collective Bargaining in Baseball." Industrial Relations Research Association Series. *Proceedings of the Twenty-Ninth Annual Winter Meeting.* Atlantic City, N.J., 1976, pp. 317-323.

Scully, Gerald W. "Pay and Performance in Major League Baseball." *The American Economic Review,* December 1974, pp. 915-930.

Seitz, Peter. "Are Professional Sports Sports or Business? or How Much Would You Pay for Catfish Hunter?" Industrial Relations Research Association Series. *Proceedings of the Twenty-Ninth Annual Winter Meeting.* Atlantic City, N.J., 1976, pp. 324-328.

Slusher, Howard S. "Sport: A Philosophical Perspective." *Law and Contemporary Problems* 38 (1973):129.

Smith, Robert. "Baseball Needs a New Pitch." *Look,* February 18, 1969, p. 74.

Sobel Lionel S. "Television Sports Blackouts: Private Rights vs. Public Policy." *Los Angeles Bar Bulletin,* March 1973, pp. 169-188.

Sosnick, Stephen H. "A Critique of Concepts of Workable Competition." *Quarterly Journal of Economics,* August 1958, pp. 380-423.

"The Super Bowl and the Sherman Act: Professional Team Sports and the Antitrust Laws." *Harvard Law Review* 81 (1967):418.

Weill, Jay R. "Depreciation of Player Contracts—The Government Is Ahead at the Half." *Taxes,* October 1975, pp. 581-591.

"Who Says Baseball Is Like Ballet?" *Forbes,* April 1, 1971, pp. 24-32.

Wise, Gordon L. "The Business of Major League Baseball as a Spectator Sport." *Bulletin of Business Research.* Ohio State University, Center for Business and Economic Research. October 1973, pp. 1-3, 6-7.

Zeidenberg, Leonard. "The Biggest Game in Town for the Networks." *Broadcasting,* September 22, 1975, pp. 37-50

Also selected articles from *Sports Illustrated, The Sporting News, Fortune, Forbes,* and many newspapers too numerous to list individually.

Index

Index

About the Authors

Jesse W. Markham graduated from the University of Richmond in 1941 and received the Ph.D. in economics from Harvard University in 1949. From 1949 until 1953 he taught at Vanderbilt University and then moved to Princeton University, where he remained for 15 years. Professor Markham joined the faculty of the Harvard Graduate School of Business Administration in 1968 and in 1972 was elected to the Charles E. Wilson professorship.

Professor Markham's professional experience has been extensive. During the 1950s he spent a year as a chief economist for the Federal Trade Commission. He also chaired the Department of Commerce Task Force on Marketing and Competition; testified frequently as an expert on federal antitrust and antimerger laws before the Senate Subcommittee on Antitrust Laws; served as U.S. delegate to the Organization for European Economic Cooperation and Development; and was one of two economists appointed to the American Bar Association's Commission to study the Federal Trade Commission. In addition, he wrote extensively on the economic effects of market structure, and his articles have appeared in such journals as the *American Economic Review*, the *Southern Economic Journal*, the *Journal of Farm Economics*, and the *Columbia Law Review*. His most recent book is *Horizontal Divestiture and the Petroleum Industry*, coauthored with Tony Hourihan and Francis Sterling (1977).

Paul V. Teplitz is vice-president and director of Cambridge Research Institute, a management consulting firm in Cambridge, Massachusetts. With a background in economic and industry analysis, he has worked with corporate clients in regulatory proceedings and antitrust litigation. He now consults in the areas of corporate strategy, organization, and policies.

Dr. Teplitz graduated from the Massachusetts Institute of Technology in 1962 and received the doctorate in business administration from Harvard University in 1969. Prior to joining the Cambridge Research Institute, he worked in the office of the president at MIT and at the MIT-Harvard Joint Center for Urban Studies. His books include *Urban Analysis* (coauthor), *America's Housing Needs: 1970 to 1980* (coauthor), and *Trends Affecting the U.S. Banking System*.